D0699007

"I have known Don Ostrom since we pioneered our church in Seattle in 1992. Don and his wife, Marlene, helped us in the planting of the church and quickly became some of our closest friends and confidants in the ministry. Within just a few years, Don was ordained as an elder in our church and has blessed us in countless ways.

"In the years I have known Don personally, and from the prior years of having known of his reputation, I have known him to be a man of the highest character and integrity. At no time has he ever used his wealth or influence as a means of manipulation or control. Quite the opposite; Don has always been careful to bless, to help, and to humbly serve our church and help extend the kingdom of God around the world.

"Because Don has been a missionary, we have traveled together to many nations, preached together, and have been used to bless many other churches and ministries. The message of this amazing book is a small reflection of the life that has been lived before us. I have had the privilege of a front-row seat in watching how God has used this great man of faith. You will experience the same privilege as you read the amazing stories included here. They will bless and stretch your faith to do more for the Lord and His kingdom.

"As a pastor, I have taught the principle of 'prosperity with a purpose.' As one of our elders and ministers in The City Church, Don Ostrom has demonstrated this fundamental principle of faith. While Don and Marlene have been blessed in many material ways, what most people do not realize is that they have sown literally millions of dollars into mission fields and churches around the world. Now those who read this outstanding book will more fully understand the message behind the man, and the purpose behind the prosperity.

"The book you hold in your hands has the potential to transform your faith and change your life. May the Lord bless you richly as you read."

—Wendell Smith
Senior Pastor, The City Church of Seattle

"My longtime friend, Don Ostrom, from his heart and from his many years of experience in the commercial world, does a masterful presentation in this book. He endeavors to show the difference between materialistic prosperity and biblical prosperity. Believe me, there is a great difference between the two.

"Materialism takes, and takes, and takes, and takes some more. It is based on greed, avarice, and covetousness. On the other hand, biblical prosperity has a different focus. God pours blessings into us, through us, and out of us, enabling us to be blessed and also to bless others.

"Generosity is the key to prosperity. This issue of living in a realm of surplus blessing was decided for me when I read J.B. Phillip's translation of 2 Corinthians 9:11 in *The New Testament in Modern English,* which says, 'The more you are enriched the more scope will there be for generous giving.' Reading Don Ostrom's book can help you discover the life of overflowing generosity and how to attain it. You'll be blessed, *big time*, reading this book."

—Dick Mills, DST and DT
Dick Mills Ministry

"The principles and strategies in this book are powerful and can cause you to break out to new levels of prosperity."

—Bob Harrison
President, Harrison International Seminars

"I have known Don for many years, both as a businessman and a Christian leader. I believe this book will provide you with some keys to help you become a success in life."

—Kenneth W. Hagin
President, Kenneth Hagin Ministries

MILLIONAIRE

IN THE PEW

MILLIONAIRE
IN THE PEW

*Keys to Faith for Prosperity
and Freedom from Poverty*

Don Ostrom

Tulsa, Oklahoma

MILLIONAIRE IN THE PEW
© 2004 by Don Ostrom

Published by Insight Publishing Group
8801 S. Yale, Suite 410
Tulsa, OK 74137
918-493-1718

All rights reserved. No part of this book may be reproduced or transmitted in any form or by any means, electronic or mechanical, including photocopying and recording, or by an information storage and retrieval system, without permission in writing from the author.

Unless otherwise noted, all Scripture quotations are taken from the King James Version of the Bible. Scripture quotations marked NKJV are taken from the *Holy Bible: New King James Version*, © 1979, 1980, 1982 by Thomas Nelson, Inc., Publishers. Scripture quotations marked NIV are from the *New International Version*, © 1960, 1962, 1963, 1968, 1971, 1972, 1973, 1975, 1977, 1995 by the Lockman Foundation. Used by permission. Scripture quotations marked NAS are from the *New American Standard Bible*, © 1960, 1962, 1963, 1968, 1971, 1972, 1973, 1975, 1977, 1995 by The Lockman Foundation. Used by permission. Scripture quotations marked AMP are taken from *The Amplified Bible, Old Testament*, © 1965, 1987 by Zondervan Corporation. *New Testament*, © 1958, 1987 by The Lockman Foundation. Used by permission.

ISBN 1-932503-21-8
Library of Congress catalog card number: 2004105738

Printed in the United States of America

DEDICATION

I gratefully dedicate this book to
the "queen" of my home, Marlene Ostrom;
and to Dan, Doug, Larry, and Paul,
my four "almost perfect" sons
who have never given me heartache or sorrow,
and who have brought great joy to my heart.
They love God, and I love them and their beautiful wives,
Kim, Cindy, Laine, and Stephanie.
May they carry this message to their generation.

Contents

Foreword

Preface

Acknowledgments

Introduction: You Can Have Millionaire Faith

Notes

FOREWORD

The following comments were written to the author after Dr. Cole had seen a draft of the book and before Dr. Cole went home to his reward:

"Don Ostrom is my friend, and you will discover as you read this book that he is yours also. He is not just practicing what he preaches, but is teaching what he has practiced. Don is a mature, principled, wise, experienced, godly man. What he has written comes from a life filled with dependence on God. I recommend Don's book not just for reading, but for living."

—Dr. Edwin Louis Cole
Founder of Christian Men's Network,
Author, and International Lecturer

PREFACE

It takes a bit of boldness to talk about financial prosperity. The word *prosperity* is avoided in many Christian circles, and even in general society there is a negative attitude toward those who seem prosperous and successful.

Because so many people live in poverty, those who intellectualize often lay guilt upon those who have much. Consequently, people have advised me not to use the word *prosperity* in the title of my book. They suggested that I use some other words so I don't turn people away from my message, but prosperity is my message, and it is the message of the gospel.

Imagine avoiding prosperity. Avoiding prosperity destroys faith. It encourages poverty and negates the power of the gospel of Jesus Christ.

Having been in sixty-nine countries of this world, I have seen poverty at its worst. I have also seen luxury beyond most human conception. My heart has gone out to those in need, and I have given millions of dollars to help those who are poor. Yet, my small amount of money has been like a tiny drop in a large bucket of need.

I realize that huge sums of money can be a blessing or a curse. Let's face it: money is power. It can be used to bribe for influence, or it can be distributed to those in need without any strings attached. In the country of my missionary calling, the Philippines, I have blessed many pastors and churches with finances that God has made available to me. At the same time, in my limited knowledge, I have hurt others because they felt ignored or left out. I don't blame them for the way they felt; I would have felt the same way.

How do we cope with the criticism of being prosperous and the temptation to misuse the blessing of wealth? What makes the difference between those who prosper for God's glory and those who gain wealth for selfish purposes? Why do some people reach the heights of financial success, while others never seem to get anywhere near it?

I am convinced that acquiring wealth and using it for good requires revelation. Maintaining godly wealth takes an inner, positive understanding of God's desire and plan that goes beyond an intellectual rationale.

So, what produces that revelation? The answer is a thorough understanding of God's nature and His plan for mankind. The only way that we can grasp that revelation is to study the heart of God. Both the intent of God's heart and His plan for us are revealed in the Holy Scriptures, the Bible. Yet, a majority of churches ignore the subject of God's desire to prosper His people.

Many churches seem to fear teaching on the subject of prosperity, but I became free of poverty as I began to see the key to escape from its destructive clutches. My understanding of God's plan to bless people with wealth and the devil's plan to kill, steal, and destroy God's blessings came only after diligent, painstaking study of this subject in the Bible.

Many Christians have been taught prosperity and know the Scriptures, but they still don't prosper. Why not? They have ignored the foundational principles of living a blessed and sanctified life such as faith, holiness, and purity, or they simply have not acted on the truth that has been revealed to them.

I know that it takes repetition to establish any truth in a life: "Faith comes by hearing, and hearing by the word of God" (Romans 10:17 NKJV). Hence, this book. In it I teach, exhort, and illustrate scriptural principles through the lessons I have learned in life that have convinced me that God wants to prosper His people. I desire to liberate your mind from negative, damnable fear and doubt. My desire is to destroy the power of guilt over financial blessings in your life and see you prosper for His purpose.

ACKNOWLEDGMENTS

My wife, Marlene, spent much time and effort to help produce this book. She has been my one and only partner for forty-nine years. She is full of life and laughter, and she is absolutely special to me. Her wit and genuineness have kept me in balance in life.

Not to be forgotten are many friends who kept asking, "Why don't you write a book?" They kept urging me to finish when I was ready to give up. Thanks to you all for your encouragement. My special thanks to Jude Fouquier for the title of the book.

Jim and Cris Bolley gave me the final hope of a book by editing it for me to my satisfaction. Thank God for their gift.

It is also an honor to acknowledge the men who have influenced my life and faith over the years:

Kenneth Hagin, Sr., invited me to serve on his board of advisors in 1980. I was privileged to sit on that board for twenty years; his life and books took me out of tradition and unbelief. Though he is now in heaven, the spirit of faith he imparted is alive.

T. L. Osborn held a crusade for us in Davao City, Philippines in 1960. That crusade turned my life around. Seeing thousands coming to Jesus opened my eyes to understand what simple faith can accomplish.

I am grateful to have been in five countries with John Osteen, who had a heart for souls. John also held a crusade in the Philippines, and he helped me to understand the charismatic move of the seventies and eighties.

Demos Shakarian and I were close friends; we traveled to many countries together. I learned love from Demos as I watched him include everyone in his circle of friends.

Shortly after Demos passed on to heaven, Dr. Edwin Cole urged me to help reach more men with the message of the gospel. Dr. Cole had the ability to bring out the best in me; he taught me to be a man, not a wimp. His many books are invaluable for men. I miss him now.

In more recent years, Bob Harrison has inspired me with his enthusiasm and creativity. I have been on his board for years, attending eighteen of his Hawaiian seminars. He has motivated me to change and expect increase in my life.

I would also like to express my gratitude to my pastor, Wendell Smith, and his wife, Gini, who have given loving support to Marlene and me. Pastor Wendell has inspired and encouraged my faith, and has covered us with prayer for twelve years at The City Church. Pastor Wendell became the great encourager in my life, and his ministry added some missing principles of stability. He visited the Philippines with me several times, and chose to undergird and strengthen my work there. His practice of stepping out in faith and his spirit of generosity have had an immense impact on my life.

INTRODUCTION

You Can Have Millionaire Faith

When I was a teenager, I saw a man drive to our church in a beautiful shiny new Cadillac. I wondered, *What is he doing at church?* I had been told that money was the root of all evil, so I thought if a person was spiritual and close to God, he couldn't have money. I had often looked at people with money and wished I had some too, but I dared not attempt to acquire wealth for fear it would destroy me. Consequently, I never dreamed that one day I would become a millionaire. Nor did I imagine that I would be telling this miraculous story of events and personal experiences that have given me the opportunity to pour millions of dollars into God's work.

In my early years, my thoughts were always of shortage. I hoarded the money I earned from my father's nursery business. Every dollar Dad paid me for shoveling dirt, I hid in a little box, refusing to spend any of it. A stingy spirit became a stronghold in my life.

Later, I realized that I was a picture of the poverty-stricken man described in the book of Proverbs: "One man gives freely, yet gains even more; another withholds unduly, but comes to poverty" (Proverbs 11:24 NIV).

My thoughts were full of negativity. I was headed down the road to a life of lack and shortage. It never entered my mind that God wanted to prosper me for a purpose. My religious traditions had taught me that to be poor was to be "godly."

Many Christians have succumbed to the idea that it is wrong to make money, believing that money should not be desired if they want to be recognized as spiritual. To some, *profit* has become a dirty word. Such believers seem afraid to prosper, fearing what people will say about them.

But God said, "If you are willing and obedient, you will eat the best from the land" (Isaiah 1:19 NIV). Often Christians want to be obedient, but they are not willing to risk criticism from others. Some people criticize us when we prosper, and Satan uses this public disapproval as a weapon of fear to keep us from receiving God's reward.

I am writing this book to establish your faith so that you will not yield to the fear of having money. Likewise, you must not belittle the importance of money. Don't look upon money as unspiritual. Money is important to God; in His Word He said, "And you shall remember the LORD your God, for it is He who gives you power to get wealth, that He may establish His covenant which He swore to your fathers, as it is this day"(Deuteronomy 8:18 NKJV).

God planned for our prosperity by giving us the ability to produce wealth. As a youth I didn't see or understand this truth. I was bound in unbelief and fear. In order to receive the financial miracles that God had available for me, the stronghold of poverty thinking had to be broken in my life.

Satan will do his best to keep strongholds of negative thinking in our minds. He wants us to be poor and sick. He doesn't want us to support the church, or to give to missionaries, or gospel radio and TV. He wants us to be so strapped financially that we can hardly pay our bills or buy food for our family. He wants us focused on a need for money and worried about shortages. This book is intended to expose his strategies and lies.

This is not a book promoting high-powered techniques, motivational insights, or Madison Avenue methods. I am a businessman. I am also a pastor. My desire is to honor God by sharing truths and principles that will help you.

When I teach on the stewardship of godly wealth, I always stress the importance of motives. The Word makes it clear that "no one can serve two masters; for either he will hate the one and love the other, or else he will be loyal to the one and despise the other. You cannot serve God and mammon"(Matthew 6:24 NKJV). (I will share more on this subject in chapter 2.)

Our attitude toward money should be positive. God wants us to have money. As Christians, we are to see money as power put into our hands to spread the gospel throughout the world. Jesus said that we are to "go therefore and make disciples of all the nations, baptizing them in the name of the Father and of the Son and of the Holy Spirit, teaching them to observe all things that I have commanded you" (Matthew 28:19-20 NKJV).

Can we go into all nations without money to travel and pay expenses? No! It takes money for transportation, lodging, and food.

I have used my money to share the life-giving power of the gospel of Jesus Christ in sixty-nine countries. It was a revelation to me that money could be used for the kingdom of God instead of for selfish gain. I had not expected my business to prosper. In fact, I felt *guilty* for having money, even though I had inherited it (that story I will also share later in the book).

At one point, I had even felt I should sell everything and give all our money to missions just to get rid of my guilt, but the Lord worked to renew my mind. He replaced my guilt with this shocking revelation: *I began to see that there is a godly reason to prosper.*

You will notice that many of the Scriptures in this book are written out in the endnotes, rather than simply referred to throughout this study. I have purposely included entire verses that should become foundations of faith for your financial miracles. To me the Bible is *life!* God's Word is more powerful than any of my words. So, even though it is easy to skip over these verses, *please take time to read and meditate on the Scriptures that are included in this work.*

In this book, I will give further explanation to what God's Word says about wealth and the reward He places on obedience. I will also discuss the difference between the tithe and offerings, and illustrate what you can expect in return if you invest in God-directed businesses.

Is it good to have lots of money? Yes and no. It depends on our attitudes and the values we place on having wealth. In the business world it is understood that it takes money to make money; therefore money is a vital, all-important commodity. Even the parable that Jesus told of the master who gave his three servants one, two, and five talents respectively (probably about $1,000, $2,000, and $5,000) shows that financial gain comes through the process of wise investments. This is why a godly attitude toward money is critical.

What people do with their money is a very good indicator of where their core values lie. Their checkbooks and their calendar schedules are pretty good indicators of whether they are serving God or money. What they do with their money speaks of who and what has priority in their lives.

If people work day and night to make money, and it consumes their time and energy, then to them money is harmful. Money is their misplaced source of confidence if they save and save because they fear "a rainy day," or if they think that hoarding it will give them a sense of peace or security. On the other hand, if people have an abundance of money and use it to help the poor and to expand the kingdom of God, to them money is good. The more, the better.

I will show you that it is not a sin for you to have money. But it is a sin when money has you. How can you know if money has you? Let me answer that question right now: If you don't tithe and give generously with the funds God has given you, then money has control of you.

There are many people in this world who have made lots of money. Some have become millionaires, but their lives are full of heartache, stress, hurt, bitterness, and family disasters. They are not enjoying true prosperity.

What good is it then to have money? The answer is simple: money can be used to bless not only the one who possesses it but many others as well. I am an example of this truth. I am enjoying a rich, full life of true prosperity as I bless others with the same blessing that God has blessed me.

As you read of my dramatic, life-changing experiences in this book, you will see that prosperity with purpose is about faith, finances, and core values. This book is not just for businesspeople. The principles in this book are valuable and productive for people in all walks of life.

There are principles in these pages that can eliminate pressure from the stress that comes when we fail to do things God's way and follow His principles. Stress comes when we rely on our own human logic rather than His wisdom. Failure can be a result of our weakness, laziness, or lack of understanding; however, I will show you how failure can also be a stepping-stone to future success.

This is a book of values and truths that I found through reading God's Word and obeying His voice. In these pages, I will share keys that have unlocked financial miracles for me. I believe that the Spirit of the Lord will reveal these same truths to you and will release you into a new dimension of spiritual and financial freedom.

Chapter One

Leave Your Comfort Zone

It was my lot as a teenager in the 1940s to grow up on a small farm, and I hated the early morning duty of milking the cow. I remember when milk went squirting on my pants as she stepped on my foot. I whacked that cow on her rump and hollered at her, "Stand still!" Dad raised pigs, chickens, rabbits, and cows, and we barely made it financially. My day always began with morning chores, regardless of cold rain or hot sunshine.

It was also my job to kill chickens or skin rabbits for our meals. After taking the bucket of milk to the house, I would pick up the axe, grab a chicken, and chop its head off. Then I would heat a pan of water, dip the chicken's carcass in the boiling steam, and pluck its feathers as I continued to moan quietly to myself, "Why do *I* have to do all this dirty stuff?"

We attended church regularly; we loved the Lord, but we never dreamed of having much money. As I have noted, I had been taught that money was the root of evil; but without money I experienced worry and sadness. Life held no purpose or excitement, and thoughts of lack and shortage plagued my young life.

Those days on Dad's small farm soon passed. After graduating from high school, I wanted to continue my education even though no one in my family had gone to college. I decided to go to a Christian college to increase my knowledge of the Bible, but one reason I was so excited about this choice in schools was that it meant leaving home and going to the big city of Seattle.

I could finally look forward to something new and different. I had no idea at that point that I would become a preacher or a businessman. I finished college four years later with a bachelor's degree. It was there that I met Marlene, a charming, vivacious girl, and we were married a year later.

Two weeks after marriage, we became the pastors of a small church in Mineral, Washington. We saw God's faithfulness to provide for our needs again and again.

We were there two years, and in that time I learned much about preaching and being a pastor. It was good experience, but I became restless. Then in the fall of 1956 we attended a missions conference—one that changed our lives forever. It was there that we listened to Gunder Olsen share his experiences as a missionary living in the Philippines for more than thirty-five years. As he was speaking, suddenly out of the blue, I clearly heard a voice saying, "Would you be willing to give your life in the Philippines?"

What? I knew it was the Lord speaking, but I was shocked. Olsen's voice faded, and I pondered what God had just asked. *Give my life?* Did He mean that I was to die there?

My first thought was for my wife, Marlene, and my young son, Dan. What would happen to them if I "gave my life" in the Philippines? However, no sooner had I had this thought than God said, softly as He had before, "Never mind them; I will take care of them."

That experience left me with a burning question. Even though God had spoken to me and told me to do so, could I actually give my life to work in the Philippines; could I really leave my country and become a missionary? It seemed impossible. I had attended a four-year Bible college, but I had not taken any courses in missions. I felt totally inadequate for what God was asking of me. Furthermore, as I was looking at a map one day, the name of Davao City, on the island of Mindanao, stood out to me. I knew that was where I was to go.

I struggled with God's question for six months. As I waited on the Lord one morning while holding meetings in Montana, I heard His voice again. He asked me, "What are you going to do about the Philippines?"

His question rattled me, and instead of simply answering, I argued with Him. "I don't have an education in missions," I reminded Him, "I'm not a strong leader. I don't have the money to move overseas." But none of my excuses fazed God.

He let me ramble on, and then He spoke some serious words that helped me make my decision quickly. He said, "Son, it is My will for you to go to the Philippines, but if you want to stay here, you may. However, if you stay, I will have to teach you some lessons."

God wanted to teach me some lessons? Oh no! That is not what any Christian wants to hear.

That day, I made a firm decision to obey God. I didn't know how to prepare, or what to do, but I said to Him, "I will go," and I meant it. I knew it was important to set a date and tell people that my family and I would be moving to the Philippines.

Small Beginnings Launch Millionaire Faith

The moment I made the decision to go, I had peace. The issue was settled. It seemed so hard to make the choice, but there is no greater joy than to make a final decision to obey God. At the time, it seemed as though it would be a great sacrifice. The unknown was frightening and formidable. But the inner sense of pleasure and peace that I had when I decided to obey God was without equal.

When you fear what God wants you to do, you are failing to realize that He is good. He has wonderful plans for you, and He knows what is best for you (see Jeremiah 29:11 NIV). From your choice of a spouse to where you go to school or what kind of business you should start, God wants to guide you and make you successful.

In fact, God wants to give you what I call "millionaire faith." This is the kind of faith that can see millions of dollars pass through your hands for His plans and purposes, but we will get to that later. The first step is simple; you have to be willing to leave your comfort zone.

One year after God spoke to me about the Philippines, we were finally ready to go to Davao City. On a cold, November night in Seattle we boarded a ship bound for Manila with our toddler, son Dan. We fully expected it to be a four-year missionary trip.

It was with great enthusiasm that we boarded the huge, three-hundred-foot-long freighter, saying good-bye to our parents and more than two hundred people from our church who had come to send us off with prayers and expressions of love.

When we stepped off the ship three weeks later, I was twenty pounds lighter because I had not been able to escape the constant tossing and turning of the ship. It had bounced like a cork on the winter waves of the Pacific Ocean, and seasickness didn't even begin to describe my misery!

Upon arrival, we walked down the ramp of the freighter, stood on the dock, and wondered where to go and what to do. In the enthusiasm of my youth, we had left America with no known contacts in the Philippines (which was incredibly foolish of me). In all of my anticipation of our new life, I had not prepared myself for the momentary dread that I felt from not having anyone to help us find our way through the language barriers when we arrived.

I loved adventure, and this was certainly it! But as we stood on that dock, doubts immediately flowed through my mind. *Should we have come to Manila?* There I was, all 120 pounds that was left of me, suddenly aware that I didn't know a soul in Manila. I thought, *Where is my pastor? Where is my supporting church? Who let me do this?*

We didn't even have a place to stay! If I had not had confidence that I was in the will of God, I am not sure I could have coped. I had a childlike faith that He was leading us, and I was determined to follow Him, but I would soon learn that God knew our servant hearts and would honor our faith in Him. I was just realizing the immensity of what I had asked my wife and two-year-old son to do as we stood in the clammy heat, on that sticky dock, when someone walked up to us and asked, "Are you the Ostroms?"

God Performs a Miracle of Provision

Shocked to hear our name, I said "That's us!" The man introduced himself as Governor Chipeco of Laguna Province. Mrs. Chipeco pinned a corsage on Marlene. The governor passed out some pesos to the customs people and whisked us away in their Mercedes to visit their gorgeous home.

Unknown to us, God had prepared an incredible miracle contact for us through a friend in the United States. Our friend had told this government official that we were coming to be missionaries. God sent the governor to greet us in our new life in the Philippines.

Although we were in the will of God, we had our share of troubles over the next few weeks. Without going into detail, let me just say that after five weeks of being in Manila, I was overjoyed that our Jeep had finally cleared customs. It seemed like a great breakthrough, but it was not without some difficulties.

When I was informed that I could get the Jeep out of customs, I went to the closest bank and withdrew enough cash to pay the import duty on the vehicle. People had warned me to beware of pickpockets, so instead of putting the money in my wallet, I divided it and put half into each of my front pockets where I felt it would be safe.

I left the bank and ran across the street to hail a jeepney, which is similar to a taxi. I climbed into the back where there were two sets of seats facing one another. Two other men came and sat with me; one sat in front and the other was at my side. I must admit that my thoughts were on finally unloading my Jeep. I was surprised when the man in front of me, who was eating peanuts, began to choke.

He stood up and leaned forward. While coughing and choking, he rested one hand on my knee and the other on the jeepney. He was spitting up on my leg, but the hand on my knee was shaking. I tried to get the driver to stop, but he didn't seem to hear.

When he did stop, I jumped off, noticing that my wallet had fallen out on the floor of the jeepney. I picked it up and instantly knew that the two men were pickpockets. I thought, *It's a good thing there was no money in my wallet!*

As I walked toward the customs gate, I took an inventory of my other pockets. I felt my left front pocket and suddenly realized the money in that pocket was gone! I was very angry. I looked around for the jeepney and its passengers, but it, along with my money, was gone.

I later learned that such offenses were not typical of most Filipinos. This kind of theft usually happens only in the big cities. At the time, all I could think of was how much I needed that money. However, even with half the cash gone, I still had enough to get the Jeep out of customs.

We had the Jeep sent to Davao City, on Mindanao, while Marlene, Dan, and I flew to the city. We landed in a small, primitive airport, not knowing a soul. There a taxi driver took us to a hotel in the area. After ten days, God gave us a wonderful house to rent. We had four hundred dollars a month from our supporting church in America to rent a house and a meeting hall, buy food and gasoline, and pay utilities and other expenses.

God blessed us, and in March of 1959, we started a church in Davao City. It opened with only two people the first night. After three years, there were more than three hundred people in attendance. We loved the work, and we loved the wonderful Filipino people who attended our church.

Our second son, Doug, was born in the Philippines. We were far from wealthy, but we had enough. We were happy!

God Stretches Our Faith to New Levels

Three years after we started our church in Davao City, a traumatic event touched our lives and changed our plans permanently. Marlene's father and sister died in a tragic plane crash in 1961, leaving her the only surviving member of the family. She left for the United States in August to begin taking care of matters regarding their estates. I reluctantly followed three months later.

Years before, I had turned down Marlene's father, Carlos Horton, when he offered to bring me into his family business. I had never felt any desire to do anything but follow the call of God on my life to be a missionary. Now with no choice in the matter, my wife and I suddenly became the owners of his businesses. We went from subsisting on God's blessings to owning two cars, a home in an elite section of Seattle, and five nursing home facilities in three different states. It was a traumatic change.

We had no idea the amount of money that God wanted to flow through us. Although we were not truly millionaires when we first inherited her father's business, we felt like we were.

Marlene and I had mixed emotions as we entered this new phase in our lives. My first concern, even a fear, had been that money would destroy my ministry. I had loved being a missionary, and I did not want to be a businessman. I knew I had been called to teach and preach the gospel. It was my life. I had heard of ministers who sold out for money, and I was determined that would not happen to me. My attitude was, "I'm not letting this business and money destroy me."

For as long as I could, I left all the business decisions to Marlene while I continued to hold meetings in churches. By that time, she was a stay-at-home mother of three children who needed her care. She was rightfully frustrated with me for my attitude. Consequently, we were in strife, which created upheaval in our home, but she must have been praying for me because things changed suddenly.

God Gets Our Attention

An evangelist came to our home church. We enjoyed his dynamic, unconventional approach to ministry, and we had time to talk with him. I explained to him that Marlene was in charge of the business because I was a minister, not a businessman.

He looked at me with shock. Suddenly, he burst out in his unconventional way and shouted, "Don Ostrom, get off your a— — and take over that business! Your wife was not designed to be in charge of a business."

That got my attention! I realized what he said was true, and I felt like a knife had been thrust right through my stomach. I made the decision to take my responsibility as a businessman.

Now I had a new challenge. A business must be managed, but I was still determined not to let the business and the money destroy me. I resented not being able to return to the Philippines. I wanted to go back, but estate matters were not settled for nearly three years. I struggled with mixed emotions, and I didn't like to be introduced as a businessman.

One day I became so frustrated that I fell to my knees in the basement of our home and cried out to the Lord, "God, what am I? Am I a preacher, or am I a businessman?" I was desperate to know His will for my life.

Then I heard God's voice clearly from within me. It was not audible, but I heard these words, "Son, it makes no difference to Me whether people call you a preacher or a businessman. Just do My will, and you will bring the highest glory to My name."

That settled it. I would just seek to please God and do His will. If He said to sell the business, I would. If He said to go back to the Philippines, I would obey. After that, I didn't care what title people gave me.

It was a new release for me. It was another step of faith, like the one I had taken when we went to Manila. This change brought another challenge to my faith. I had to get out of my "comfort zone." I knew that faith was the key, but I also knew that my faith must be in God's ability, not mine.

A Transformation Was Coming

I studied the Bible in light of my new responsibilities. I found good books on faith and financial success. I made friendships with positive, faith-filled men and women. Slowly, but surely, Satan's lies and deception about poverty began to lose their hold on my life. Marlene and I began to change our confessions, not only about money but also about ourselves.

When I was propelled into the business world, I was a novice. Immediately, Satan began his strategy to keep me from experiencing prosperity. His design was to keep me poor. A transformation was coming, but he was determined to stop it and keep me in old patterns of thinking.

In his effort to keep God's people in poverty, the devil will even quote Scripture, whispering to our thoughts, "Money will destroy you. Money is filthy lucre."[1] Then he will add, "Remember, it *is* harder for a rich man to go into the kingdom of heaven than for a camel to go through the eye of a needle."[2]

But Satan takes the Word out of context and twists it to steal its power from us. Once a person is in the kingdom of heaven through faith in Jesus Christ, it is God's will to prosper him or her financially. The psalmist declared: "Let them shout for joy and rejoice, who favor my vindication; and let them say continually, 'The LORD be magnified, who delights in the prosperity of His servant'" (Psalm 35:27 NAS).

Satan misquotes another verse by saying that money is the root of evil. That is not true. *Money* is not the root of evil; it is the *"love of money"* that breeds evil acts and greed. First Timothy 6:10 NIV makes clear this distinction: "For the love of money is a root of all kinds of evil. Some people, eager for money, have wandered from the faith and pierced themselves with many griefs."

The devil's misquotes are fuel for the fire of negative attitudes toward financial prosperity and freedom from poverty. These same lies were the foundation of disbelief that Satan once used to keep me from prospering.

In spite of all this negativity, God brought some dramatic changes to set me free from this misguided mentality. Believe me, it was quite a transition. God gave me the key truths, which I am sharing with you in this book, to empower me with a positive attitude toward financial success. These keys to millionaire faith will empower you to receive God's best for your life. In the next chapter, I will show you *why* God wants you to receive financial blessings, but without taking the first step you can never start your journey into a life of faith and abundance.

Key #1

Leave your comfort zone.

- Obedience is always the first step with God.

- Break free from the familiar, no matter how difficult it seems to do so.

- Trust that God's provision will follow your obedience.

- Don't let wealth hinder your relationship with God.

- Transformation is easier when you spend time in prayer, and know you are in God's will.

Chapter Two

Be Blessed to Be a Blessing

More than two decades ago, I decided to be a dispenser of money to help others. At first I wondered what I would do when my money ran out. But amazingly, the more I gave, the more funds came. It became a wonderful, exciting cycle. Give away; more comes. Give that away, and still more comes. Be blessed, and then be a blessing. Be a blessing, and then be blessed. I will share some of those wonderful experiences later.

My transformation from feeding a spirit of poverty to having millionaire faith began when my friend Fred Doerflein invited me to a Full Gospel Businessmen's Fellowship convention in Phoenix, Arizona. At this conference, I heard wealthy men giving their testimonies of how their money allowed them to travel to other countries to share the gospel of Jesus Christ. I had never heard businessmen share these kinds of things. I was surprised and inspired. I could easily see how their prosperity had enabled them to spread their testimonies all over the world.

As I sat with these men, I remembered God's Word, "Command those who are rich in this present age not to be haughty, nor to trust in uncertain riches but in the living God, who gives us richly all things to enjoy. Let them do good, that they be rich in good works, ready to give, willing to share, storing up for themselves a good foundation for the time to come, that they may lay hold on eternal life" (1 Timothy 6:17-19 NKJV). With this new concept for my life, I had a new purpose for prospering.

Here are some biblical declarations concerning the prosperity that God wants you to enjoy:

Carefully follow the terms of this covenant, *so that you may prosper in everything you do.* (Deuteronomy 29:9 NIV, italics mine)

Do not let this Book of the Law depart from your mouth; meditate on it day and night, so that you may be careful to do everything written in it. *Then you will be prosperous and successful.* (Joshua 1:8 NIV, italics mine)

Let them shout for joy and be glad, who favor my righteous cause; and let them say continually, "Let the LORD be magnified, *who has pleasure in the prosperity of His servant.*" (Psalm 35:27 NKJV, italics mine)

My pastor, Wendell Smith, of The City Church in Kirkland, Washington, emphasizes in his teachings the concept of "prosperity with purpose." The purpose of prosperity is to build the kingdom of God and help the poor. A characteristic of true prosperity is unselfishness; in other words, a godly and wealthy person is a generous person.

I now know the purpose of financial blessings; the wealth of God's people is to finance the work in the kingdom of God. From the wealth that God has entrusted to me, I can provide funds for the vision of my pastor and church, which includes missions, buildings, TV ministry, and feeding the poor. I now travel the world sharing Jesus, teaching God's truth, and exposing the devil's lies.

In Matthew 6:24 NKJV, Jesus said, "Ye cannot serve God and mammon," which is translated in *The Amplified Bible* as "deceitful riches, money, possessions, or whatever is trusted in." The Greek word for *mammon* implies a "confidence, i.e. wealth, personified."[1] Vine's *Expository Dictionary of New Testament Words* defines *mammon* as "riches . . . that which is to be trusted . . . derived from a Hebrew word signifying 'treasure.'"

The late Dr. Derek Prince, a Greek scholar whom I knew personally, taught this description: "Mammon is more than just money. Mammon is an evil, spiritual power that grips and enslaves men through the medium of money. That spiritual power works in the world and in the lives of millions of people."[2]

In Luke 16:10-11 NIV Jesus told His followers, "Whoever can be trusted with very little can also be trusted with much, and whoever is dishonest with very little will also be dishonest with much. So if you have not been trustworthy in handling worldly wealth, who will trust you with true riches?"

To be trusted with God's wealth, we must determine whether our desire for wealth is to advance the kingdom of God or simply to amass more "stuff." To serve mammon for material gain is the work of an evil spiritual power that grips and enslaves people through their lust for money, and it is never satisfied. It is very difficult for greed to destroy the person who tithes and gives generously to God's work.

Derek Prince went on to say, "If your life is committed to God, you will despise mammon. This attitude is not hating money, but loathing that satanic force that enslaves men and women through money. You will detest it and not let it dominate you. You cannot maintain a position of neutrality on this subject." This is a very powerful truth. I do not put my confidence in mammon, but I use my money for God's kingdom.

When Jesus commanded His disciples to go into all the world, He knew it would require finances. Have you ever tried traveling anywhere without money?

Choose the Adventure with God

As I shared in the previous chapter, God is pleased when His people prosper, so why just scrape by in life? Why live on the edge of poverty and lack? Believe for your own hundreds of dollars; then you can give hundreds. Believe for your thousands; then you can give thousands. Believe for your millions; what could you give then? God's provision is not limited. The choice to be prosperous is yours.

Pastor Casey Treat used to say, "You are not a Ping-Pong ball on the table of life. Don't let Satan call the shots and shove you around at will." If you are a child of God, you are to reign in life. Let God, who gives life to the dead and calls things that are not as though they were, call the shots for you.[3]

Focus on God's priorities for your life. Remember, money is not the goal of life. In Matthew 6:33, Jesus said to seek His kingdom and His righteousness, and all the things that require money will be given to us as well. As we focus on the proper issues of a kingdom-centered life, money will surely come into our hands.

I am not suggesting that millions of dollars will just drop from the sky. Financial prosperity doesn't just appear as we sit idle like a couch potato. Prosperity is not an accident, but neither is poverty. Both conditions are the result of personal lifestyle and choices.

Application and discipline are involved in attaining financial success. If we desire a life of success, there must also be discipline in our lives. We must demonstrate millionaire faith *before* we are trusted with wealth. As we focus on the proper issues of life, godly core values will bring success and wealth into our hands.

Here are some of the disciplines that will keep you in an adventure with God while accumulating wealth:

- Have strong faith in God's ability.
- Serve God and others no matter how wealthy you become.
- Confess the Word of God in all of your decisions.
- Pray continually; keep both systematic and spontaneous times of prayer.
- Give priority attention to your family and children.
- Submit to a pastor and a local church.
- Develop virtuous character by obeying God.
- Be generous in your giving to God's work.

These basics are priorities. They are the real values in life. With them success is inevitable.

To gain wealth from God's blessing, we must be diligent to *apply* the Word of God in our lives. Do we study God's Word because we need money or for the sake of becoming a millionaire? No! Peace with God is much more important than wealth, and there is no substitute for the discipline of our time to study the Word of God. As our knowledge of God's promises increases, our circumstances of life change to reflect His will for us.

Frankly, just a few moments of concentration on the following Scripture will verify what I just said. "If you fully obey the LORD your God and carefully follow all his commands I give you today, the LORD your God will set you high above all the nations on earth. All these blessings will come upon you and accompany you if you obey the LORD your God" (Deuteronomy 28:1-2 NIV).

Pay strict attention to the Word of God; observe and obey it, and blessings will abound. Kingdom-centered goals, not self-centeredness, bring fulfillment in life. Harmony with God brings a life full of joy. Faith thrives in an atmosphere of love and peace. Little by little, negative attitudes and negative thinking disappear as we conform to God's Word. A new outlook on life comes. We begin to see the possibilities instead of the problems. We take charge in life rather than become a victim of circumstances. It is a continual process.

Life can be a drag or a positive, exciting adventure—the choice is ours. If we establish proper priorities and core values in line with God's priorities and values, life is full of wonderful surprises; sometimes we call them "miracles." We enjoy divine appointments with people that lead to prosperous situations. Unusual financial deals come our way. We are amazed—and excited.

God Had a Surprise for Me

Many years ago, God gave me a breakthrough in my thinking. It involved the purchase of a motor home. We loved to spend time outdoors and travel with our four boys, but Marlene did not like the idea of camping in a tent or lying on the ground at night. Our neighbor offered us a fabulous deal to buy his thirty-two-foot motor home. It had low mileage, and he offered it to us for half its original price, $12,500. We wanted it, but the more I thought about it, the more I told myself no. I felt I should give that money to God for missions. I struggled between buying and giving.

As I was shaving one day, I was thinking about that vehicle. I decided that I had to give the money to God rather than spend it on a luxury item. Then, I heard a clear word from God, "Why don't you buy the motor home and give the same amount to Me?"

I thought about that for about five seconds and said to the Lord, "It's a deal!"

We bought the motor home, but we gave the same amount to the Lord. We went many places together in that motor home and had a great time of bonding with our sons as we went to camp meetings, conventions, the ocean, the mountains, and lakes. It turned out to be an excellent investment for us as a family.

If we choose the life of faith and adventure, we choose to stay connected to God's blessings; we *choose* to make the first hour of the day a time with the Lord; we *choose* to meditate on the Word of God; we *choose* to keep our joy, regardless of situation or problems; we *choose* to be unselfish. We *choose* to give our lives as servants to others; we *choose* to give financially, planting seed for a great harvest. We resolve to follow Him.

Because we know He cannot fail, we are determined to believe, to feed our faith, and starve our doubts. We are secure in God's love because we obey Him. We step out in faith, and it pleases the Lord so much. We know God will protect us because of the choices we make. When we choose the life of faith, so many good things happen that we wonder, *Why did You bless me, Lord? I didn't deserve that*. What is our response to such a good God? Simply, "Thank You, thank You, thank You!" Then our hearts go up in praise to a good and loving God.

True Prosperity Is More than Money

When the Bible says that God prospers His people, does it mean they will all be made rich? The Bible describes being "rich" in 2 Corinthians 9:8 AMP: "And God is able to make all grace (every favor and earthly blessing) come to you in abundance, so that you may always and under all circumstances and whatever the need be self-sufficient [possessing enough to require no aid or support and furnished in abundance for every good work and charitable donation]."

Rich? Kenneth Hagin said the Lord told him, "If you'll listen to Me, I will make you rich. I am not opposed to my children being rich, I am opposed to their being covetous."[4]

Are we, God's people, to be rich? You bet! Yet with a lot more than money: True prosperity includes a sense of overall well-being. The apostle John wrote, "Beloved, I pray that you may *prosper in all things* and be in health, just as your *soul* prospers" (3 John 1:2 NKJV, italics mine). True prosperity is being right with God, and it is living in good health. It is peace and joy in life. It includes having godly friends. It is belonging to a lively church. It is being loved by a pastor. It is having children who love the Lord and honor Him. This is when the soul prospers; and yes, true prosperity is having money to give to others in need. Prosperity with purpose is being able to give money for God's work.

As I write this book, I have been a successful businessman for more than forty-two years. Before that I was a pastor and missionary for six years. I still wear both hats; I am a missionary for the gospel of Christ and a businessman. Those hats function very well together as I wear them with integrity and a desire to please God.

In my lifetime, and recently with the help of my son, Doug, we have built eleven multimillion-dollar buildings to care for the elderly in various communities. I have sold some and built others. Overall, I have had dramatic successes in these years. I have experienced miserable failures as well. Those failures came only because I did not listen to God and good counsel. I was determined to do things my way!

I have had many life-changing experiences that formed my life, my character, my faith, and my goals. God made His Scriptures real to me and released me from fear and negative thinking. As I continue to share the Bible promises and personal experiences that changed my thinking, I hope you gain wisdom and grow in strength to believe God for your own prosperity.

As a businessman, I know the feeling of panic when the papers of a lawsuit are shoved at us. I know the desperate, sinking feeling when payroll is due in five days, and we don't have the money. I have been there when the payment on a building was due, and the bank account was short. It was during these times that we learned to humble ourselves, get on our knees, and cry out to God for answers.

I have been in the test, and I have come through it. Before becoming a businessman, when I was a young pastor, the day came when there was no food in our house. That morning we opened the front door, and there lay a sack of groceries. I have experienced both lack and abundance. I am not afraid to talk about the blessing of money, yet I happily live a life of faith. Both subjects are an important part of our lives.

Knowing what God has to say about faith and finances can mean the difference between fulfillment and failure. I am not ashamed of the truths and success that God has given me. He has kept His Word and blessed me financially. Money doesn't rule my life. Money is not my god. God's Word is my guide. My greatest desire is to serve with a heart of faith and a servant's attitude. That pleases Him.

I want to find God's ways and principles to serve Him. I want God's help and favor in my business. I am not ashamed of that fact. I need Him; so do you. Heaven help us if we think we are smart enough to run our lives without God's help. God is not our crutch; He is our business partner. Thank God I learned that truth long ago.

God is absolutely interested in every detail of our lives. *He has planned failure for no one.* God wants us to prosper. I learned this important truth by studying Scriptures relevant to our personal and business affairs. The Bible relates to everyday living. I hope to make this truth so clear in these next chapters that you can put them into practice in your own life.

Be blessed to be a blessing to others.

- Never, never settle for less than God's best.

- Pay strict attention to the Word of God.

- Remember, God doesn't make people sick or poor; and He defeated the one who would!

- Faith and obedience always go together.

- Keep faith in your heart and mouth.

- God didn't plan failure for you. Refusing to take risks in life will stunt your growth in faith.

Chapter Three

Estimate Your Increase

All biblical success in life centers on active faith. Dynamic faith in action really pleases God. In fact, "without faith it is impossible to please and be satisfactory to Him" (Hebrews 11:6 AMP). I am sure that the testimony of God's faithfulness in my life will inspire you to *activate* millionaire faith. I encourage you to actively serve God with your tithe and offerings, even if it defies logic.

Here is how Marlene and I took action in faith when we had been in business for only two years. It wasn't logical, but one year I felt led to estimate my income and start tithing on the amount we needed to earn.

We Estimated Our Expected Tithe

It was unusual, but we estimated the amount of income we wanted for the next year. Then, starting in January, we tithed on that amount monthly. (We estimated the income, divided it by twelve, and tithed that amount). Guess what? At the end of the year the amount of our business profit was exactly what we had estimated.

The next year we increased our estimated income, and we tithed on that increased amount each month. That year, the same thing happened: we made that income. The third year, we increased the estimate again. But something went wrong. We blew a fuse! We made far more profit than our estimated amount.

God surprised us. He is wonderfully exciting. Over the years, He has surprised us again and again.

We are saved by faith. We are healed by faith. We get answers to prayer by faith. Our finances are blessed because of faith. God blesses our homes and families because of our faith.

Focus on Faith

It makes sense to focus on the principle of faith. It should be a life quest. Our attitude should be, "I will be a person of faith. Nothing will stop me from developing strong faith. I will never stop my pursuit of faith. I am ever learning to stretch my faith."

Satan will attempt to destroy our faith. The devil hates us, and he will do anything and everything to steal, destroy, or limit our faith. If nothing else, Satan will endeavor to damage what faith we have or keep us from using it. He will use people to ridicule our faith. They may call us "super-spiritual" and tell us that we have gone too far in this matter of faith.

I want to help you develop a dynamic faith that pleases God. There is no limit to faith. As my friend, the late Dr. Edwin Cole, once said, "Faith never limits God, and God never limits faith."

We have all been given a measure of faith, but what happens with that faith depends on our understanding of the Bible and its promises. The fact is that faith comes from diligent study of the Word of God: "Faith comes from hearing the message, and the message is heard through the word of Christ" (Romans 10:17 NIV).

If you study the Word of God, faith will come. Fill yourself with faith by reading God's Word every day. Use it like a doctor's prescription. A physician tells you what to take, how much, and how often. If you follow the instructions in the prescription, you get good results. However, if you decide to only take half of the prescription, you will probably complain about the doctor and his wisdom. In other words, "Take as directed!"[1] The same is true of God's Word. We cannot get too much of the Word of God. We should digest some every day. Jesus said, "Man does not live on bread alone, but on every word that comes from the mouth of God" (Matthew 4:4 NIV).

The late faith teacher, Dr. Kenneth Hagin, once said, "Faith is grasping the unrealities of hope and bringing them into the realm of reality."[2] In other words, faith changes hope into reality. Faith acts in the face of contrary evidence. Faith counts the thing done before God has acted.

Abraham's faith pleased God. The Bible says that Abraham believed God "who gives life to the dead and calls into being that which does not exist" (Romans 4:17 NAS). Counting something done before God has acted compels Him into action. God operates on this principle of our faith.

The Bible tells us that each of us has a unique faith. "For I say, through the grace given unto me, to every man that is among you, not to think of himself more highly than he ought to think; but to think soberly, according as God hath dealt to every man the measure of faith" (Romans 12:3). If faith grows and increases, it is because we feed it, exercise it, and pursue it.

The writer of Hebrews challenged believers to learn the truths of God's Word, saying, "In fact, though by this time you ought to be teachers, you need someone to teach you the elementary truths of God's word all over again. You need milk, not solid food! Anyone who lives on milk, being still an infant, is not acquainted with the teaching about righteousness. But solid food is for the mature, *who by constant use* have trained themselves to distinguish good from evil" (Hebrews 5:12-14 NIV, italics mine).

Faith is not an accident. It is a gift of God. It is stretched and developed by certain principles *and actions*. It grows as it is used. Mix the "leaven" of faith into all areas of your life: the physical, material, and spiritual.

Jesus said, "According to your faith be it unto you" (Matthew 9:29). Your harvest is determined by your faith. Ever increasing faith means ever increasing fruit and harvest!

We can't mix faith with doubt. And we can't mix faith with mental assent. Mental assent only agrees with the Word of God in the mind, but never acts on it. I don't know about you, but I don't want to be wimpy and passive; I want an active, dynamic faith that pleases God.

A Five-Dollar Action of Faith

Believe it or not, our faith is easily tested and matured by means of money. In fact, most growth in faith involves money. God often challenges us to give when we can't see how. When we do give in faith, we soon see a miracle.

The only time that God ever told us to "prove" Him was in regard to money. He said, "Bring ye all the tithes into the storehouse, that there may be meat in mine house, and prove me now herewith, saith the LORD of hosts, if I will not open you the windows of heaven, and pour you out a blessing, that *there shall* not *be room* enough *to receive it*" (Malachi 3:10).

As a young Bible student, I decided to believe God's Word in this area that greatly tested my faith. While I was attending Northwest College in Seattle, a missionary from the Philippines came to chapel one morning and shared his vision. He gave an opportunity for us to give financially.

I felt I should give five dollars, but as a student I was always short of money. It was one of my first experiences in giving, and it doesn't sound like much now, but a few dollars bought quite a bit in the 1950s. (That five dollars would be like fifty dollars in today's economy.) I did put the five dollars in the offering; however, it was with only a little faith and many thoughts of shortage because of it.

Why is it that every time we give, we think it will mean that we will have to do without something we need? I know better now, but giving those five dollars back then seemed to mean that I would suffer from having less money the next week. I soon learned that my thinking was wrong.

Several weeks later, a fellow employee asked about my schooling. I think he could see I needed extra funds. He invited me to come to his apartment, saying, "I have a suit that I don't use. Let's see if it will fit you." Sure enough it fit me perfectly. He said, "It's yours."

At the time I didn't make any connection between his gift and the giving of my five dollars. Later, the Lord showed me that the suit was saved for me because I gave. I began to see that the way out of lack and shortage of money was to *give* money to the Lord. I learned that the best way to save money is by giving to God. Giving to God's work is the best investment.

Action Identifies Faith That Pleases God

As I studied the Word, I was able to renew my mind to agree with God's promises. The following principles of faith and their corresponding Scriptures helped loose me from poverty thinking to millionaire faith:

- *Knowing God produces faith.*

    "But the people who know their God shall be strong, and carry out great exploits." (Daniel 11:32, NKJV)

    Looking unto Jesus the author and finisher of our faith. (Hebrews 12:2)

- *Meditating on the Word produces faith.*

  "This book of the law shall not depart from your mouth, but you shall meditate on it day and night, so that you may be careful to do according to all that is written in it; for then you will make your way prosperous, and then you will have success." (Joshua 1:8 NAS)

  But his [the righteous person's] delight is in the law of the LORD, and in His law he meditates day and night. He shall be like a tree planted by the rivers of water, that brings forth its fruit in its season, whose leaf also shall not wither; and whatever he does shall prosper. (Psalm 1:2-3 NKJV)

  "Therefore keep the words of this covenant, and do them, that you may prosper in all that you do." (Deuteronomy 29:9 NKJV)

- *Confessing the Word produces faith.*

  Let us hold fast the confession of our hope without wavering, for He who promised is faithful. (Hebrews 10:23 NKJV)

  Death and life are in the power of the tongue: and they that love it shall eat the fruit thereof. (Proverbs 18:21)

  If you confess with your mouth the Lord Jesus and believe in your heart that God has raised Him from the dead, you will be saved. For with the heart one believes unto righteousness, and with the mouth confession is made unto salvation. (Romans 10:9-10 NKJV)

So that we may boldly say, The Lord is my helper, and I will not fear what man shall do unto me. (Hebrews 13:6)

- *Godly living produces faith.*

  Beloved, if our heart does not condemn us, we have confidence toward God. And whatever we ask we receive from Him, because we keep His commandments and do those things that are pleasing in His sight. (1 John 3:21-22 NKJV)

  Therefore, having these promises, beloved, let us cleanse ourselves from all filthiness of the flesh and spirit, perfecting holiness in the fear of God. (2 Corinthians 7:1 NKJV)

- *Acting on the Word produces faith.*

  By faith Abraham obeyed when he was called to go out to the place which he would receive as an inheritance. And he went out, not knowing where he was going. (Hebrews 11:8 NKJV)

- *Obedience produces faith.*

  But someone will say, "You have faith, and I have works." Show me your faith without your works, and I will show you my faith by my works. (James 2:18 NKJV)

- *Experiencing miracles produces faith.*

  Then the seventy returned with joy, saying, "Lord, even the demons are subject to us in Your name." And He said to them, "I saw Satan fall like lightning from heaven. Behold, I give you the authority to trample on serpents and scorpions, and over all the power of the enemy, and nothing shall by any means hurt you." (Luke 10:17-19 NKJV)

Active—Not Passive—Faith Is the Key

Be determined to get what God promised in His Word for you. Make up your mind that you will not be denied any good thing that God has promised for you (see Psalm 84:11). Be aggressive. Boldly say, "I will not be denied the rights and privileges given to me in the Bible. Satan, flee. I resist you. I reject your lies." Take dominion over him (see James 4:7 and 1 Peter 5:9).

Faith matures slowly. It is not an instantaneous thing. We are to study, meditate, and consume the Word of God day after day, consistently. We must actively decide to get the Word of God in our spirits. We should actively fill our minds with His promises. We need to program knowledge of His truth into our hearts.

The Bible, or God's written Word, is sometimes called *logos*, while His personal revelation spoken to our hearts is referred to as His *rhema*. What is the result if we fill our hearts with His logos, His written Word? Faith comes. It comes almost subconsciously. Then when our heart is filled with God's written logos, a specific, inspired instruction, a *rhema*, comes to us when we need answers. In other words, a "knowing" from God's Word comes to build more faith in us.[3]

(As I explained in the introduction of this book, I have deliberately inserted entire Scripture passages in this book. *Don't pass over them; they are more important than my words.* If you skipped over the previous verses, stop and read them before you move on to the next chapter.)

Once the Word of God is in our spirit, we know our rights, our benefits, and our privileges. We become strong in faith. We become bold as a lion. We take action and say to the devil, "Oh no you don't. You're not getting away with that. Leave with your sickness. Get your hands off my money. I am not a beggar. I am a child of the King, and He takes care of me. Shut up, Satan! Leave, in Jesus' name."

Remember, *you are never at the mercy of the devil if you are full of the Word of God.*

Tithe from your estimated increase.

- Use your God-given "beginning" faith.

- Feed and exercise your faith to make it grow.

- Know God's promises: Presumption is pseudofaith and has no foundation in the Word of God.

- Faith is an action, not an accident.

- Never limit God.

- Development of faith should be the great quest of your life.

Chapter Four

Just Get Up and Grow!

Marlene and I have focused on building our faith for more than forty-five years. We attend conferences that build our faith, not tear it down. Sure it costs money to fly places and pay for hotel rooms, but growing in faith is a priority in our lives. We spend money on books and tapes that build our faith. Our investment of time and money has paid great dividends. Our faith is strong. We are continually growing.

We need strong faith in these fast-paced days when many changes are taking place. We are determined to hang on to the Word of God like a bulldog with a juicy bone. In so doing, we find that God honors that kind of faith.

God loves active faith. Don't let go. The key to ever-increasing faith is to devour the Bible through studying, reading good books on spiritual subjects, and listening to good biblical teaching. If your faith is small, search for books and messages on faith. The more you understand faith, the more you will want to learn faith. Listen to messages that teach about active "get-up-and-go" faith.

Active Faith

Active faith comes by allowing the Word of God to saturate our beings. Faith is more than a repertoire of memorized Scriptures that we quote. Faith is the Word coming alive in our spirits. Faith *knows* that all things are possible, regardless of the circumstances.

Active faith believes the Bible. Active faith is "hooking up with God."

Abraham had active faith. God said to him, "Get thee out of thy country, and from thy kindred, and from thy father's house, unto a land *that I will shew thee"* (Genesis 12:1, italics mine). Active faith gets up and goes, and Abraham got up and went, not yet knowing where he was supposed to go (see Hebrews 11:8).

We are Abraham's seed. We are to "get up and go." We are not to sit in an easy chair and wait for something to happen. We are heirs to the promises that God made to Abraham. The Word says, "And if ye be Christ's, then are ye Abraham's seed, and heirs according to the promise" (Galatians 3:29). We are to be like Caleb, who believing God's promises were true, said, "Let us go up at once, and possess it [the land given to the Israelites by God]; for we are well able to overcome it" (Numbers 13:30).

Those who look only at the natural circumstances, stand around complaining and mumbling in unbelief. But as heirs to Abraham's promise, we are to eliminate small thinking. We are to change our thought life to conform it to the mind of Christ.[1] We are to stop our self-imposed limitations. As faith-filled believers, we are not limited to logic. We broaden our scope beyond the familiar. We step out of our comfort zone.

When God told Abraham he would have a son, Abraham changed his concentration on having no son. He stopped focusing on Sarah's age. He quit thinking about the seventeen years with no children (see Hebrews 11:11). God told Abraham, "I am the Almighty God; walk before me, and be thou perfect. And I will make my covenant between me and thee, and will multiply thee exceedingly" (Genesis 17:1-2).

God had spoken. Abraham started thinking increase. He began to think multiplication. Abraham believed God: "He staggered not at the promise of God through unbelief; but was strong in faith, giving glory to God; and being fully persuaded that, what he had promised, he was able also to perform. And therefore it was imputed to him for righteousness" (Romans 4:20-22).

Abraham left family, friends, and home to follow God. He stepped out. It made God happy. His faith was rewarded. "Therefore, the promise comes by faith, so that it may be by grace and may be guaranteed to all Abraham's offspring—not only to those who are of the law but also to those who are of the faith of Abraham. He is the father of us all" (Romans 4:16 NIV). We are heirs to the promise of Abraham. We are to stop looking at the natural, trying to figure out how God will make His promises come to pass.

We Moved in Faith in Glenwood, Iowa

When I was young in business, my wife and I decided to build a 160-bed facility in Glenwood, a small town in the Midwest. We knew it was God's will to fill that community's need for nursing home beds. We started drawing plans and bought land. Would it be successful? The cost was a huge amount, $450,000. We believed it would be a success, but it was an act of faith on our part to proceed with the plans for such an expensive project.

Miraculously, we got financing, and one year later opened the shiny new facility. Upon opening, our faith was challenged. Funds were short. There were many empty beds, but we continued to believe. We prayed in faith. We cried out to God in desperation. In a few months, we were in the "black" financially. Our act of faith was rewarded. It had to be a miracle, because we were so young and inexperienced.

Blessings and miracles await those who believe without seeing. Faith believes the Word of God before seeing any manifestation of its promise. Don't have the doubting-Thomas kind of faith.

Throw Off Doubt

The disciple Thomas was full of doubt after the resurrection of Jesus. His faith was dependent on his natural, physical senses. The following passage tells how he wanted to *see and touch* the hands of Jesus before he would believe that Jesus was alive.

> Now Thomas, called the Twin, one of the twelve, was not with them when Jesus came. The other disciples therefore said to him, "We have seen the Lord." So he said to them, "Unless I see in His hands the print of the nails, and put my finger into the print of the nails, and put my hand into His side, I will not believe."
>
> And after eight days His disciples were again inside, and Thomas with them. Jesus came, the doors being shut, and stood in the midst, and said, "Peace to you!" Then He said to Thomas, "Reach your finger here, and look at My hands; and reach your hand here, and put it into My side. Do not be unbelieving, but believing."
>
> And Thomas answered and said to Him, "My Lord and my God!"
>
> Jesus said to him, "Thomas, because you have seen Me, you have believed. Blessed are those who have not seen and yet have believed." (John 20:24-29 NKJV)

Remember, you can have faith in your inheritance; as a believer in Christ, you are the seed of Abraham: "And if ye be Christ's, then are ye Abraham's seed, and heirs according to the promise" (Galatians 3:29). Keep this fact in your heart to burn as fuel for your faith even though you can't see and touch God's miracles at this time.

The Word says: "Christ hath redeemed us from the curse of the law, being made a curse for us: for it is written, Cursed is every one that hangeth on a tree: that the blessing of Abraham might come on the Gentiles through Jesus Christ; that we might receive the promise of the Spirit through faith" (Galatians 3:13-14).

Don't allow low expectations. Lack of expectancy is evidence of little faith. Faithlessness is almost irreverent. The element of expectancy is the basic DNA of faith. Things seen are temporary and subject to change (see 2 Corinthians 4:18 NIV).

Faith is not *trying* to believe; faith never tries. Faith speaks. Faith commands. Faith expects. Faith receives. Faith refuses to compromise. Faith praises. Faith doesn't waver. Faith wins!

Just get up and grow!

- Keep God first in your life. Often this involves the giving of money.

- Give in difficult times to prove you are "seeking first the kingdom of God."

- Don't allow conditions and circumstances to affect your faith.

- Believe God even when you can't see His answers.

- Don't be a "doubting Thomas," simply _trying_ to believe. Accept God's Word as fact.

Chapter Five

Feed Faith and Starve Doubt

"Faith comes by hearing, and hearing by the word of God" (Romans 10:17 NKJV). I add, faith comes by *continual* hearing, and hearing, and hearing—then faith comes. So if faith pleases God, we should develop it.

The Word says, "But without faith it is impossible to please Him, for he who comes to God must believe that He is, and that He is a rewarder of those who diligently seek Him" (Hebrews 11:6 NKJV). If faith pleases God then unbelief is a thief because it robs us from the reward that is given to those who seek Him.

If we are robbed by unbelief, then we should focus on building the faith that pleases God who meets our needs. The more we *function and act* on faith in God's Word, the more we understand it.

Exercising faith is like using the computer. Remember the first time you tried to use the computer? You probably wondered how it worked. You may have tried to figure it out, guessing at what to do. But, as you studied it and practiced using it, you finally became more relaxed and confident with its ability to assist you in what you needed to do. Once you understand the benefits of the computer, you not only use it, you depend on it and actually enjoy using it.

Living the life of faith requires practice. You try to understand how faith works, but at first it seems elusive.

Every step of faith, and the ensuing miracles, gives you more confidence to use faith again.

By using faith, you eventually understand that God is committed to His Word. He will not fail you. He is a faithful God. The more you act in faith and obedience, the more you understand God, and the more you understand faith. Conversely, if you hold back from using your faith because of fear or logic, you will never fully comprehend how faith works.

A Second Challenge with Five Dollars

My continued journey into faith and financial freedom again involved only five dollars; it occurred when Marlene and I became pastors of the church in Washington state. We were tithing from our small income of $160 a month.

One day the Lord impressed me to send five dollars to a pastor in Oregon. I tried to explain to the Lord that *I had already tithed.* Not only that, I had a car payment due the next week. How could I do what He said? (As if the Lord didn't know all this.) Once I finally took the big step of faith and mailed the money to the pastor, I felt so good. I had obeyed the Lord.

We were surprised when the very next week we received a check in the mail from an electrician friend who had earned overtime on an unexpected emergency on Sunday. He wrote, "The Lord told me to send you the money I earned that day." It was a check for twenty dollars! Remember, this was in 1955, and twenty dollars would be like two hundred dollars today. The amount is not important, but the principle is the same.

This was a stepping-stone in learning faith that led to our handling millions of dollars, but I didn't know it at the time. Later, I realized that the gift to us of twenty dollars was a fulfillment of Luke 6:38 NIV: "Give, and it will be given to you. A good measure, pressed down, shaken together and running over, will be poured into your lap. For with the measure you use, it will be measured to you."

I received: (1) a good measure, (2) pressed down, (3) shaken together, and (4) running over *four times* what I had given! That small beginning directed my life toward financial freedom.

Giving Is a Stepping-Stone to Financial Abundance

I had learned another great lesson in faith. It was a stepping-stone to our financial freedom. Marlene and I were struggling financially as we served as pastors in that little church. We had been tithing from our small income, but we learned a valuable lesson by giving more than our tithe. We learned that "it is more blessed to give than to receive" (Acts 20:35).

We were in need of a better car. I was driving an old 1946 Dodge, and it was failing. Then an exciting thing happened. We received five hundred dollars in the mail. I was thinking that now we could get a better car.

The next day I heard a little voice inside me say, "Give the whole five hundred dollars away." I started to say, "Get out of here, Satan," but I knew it was the voice of the Lord. (The devil will never tell us to give to and bless others.)

Marlene agreed with me. (By the way, agreement with your spouse is important so both of you can share in the joy.) We felt impressed to give three hundred dollars of it to a new pastor who was coming to a nearby town. We prepared a box of food and wrote a check to him for that amount. I felt like a millionaire.

We drove to the church in Morton, Washington. We asked a lady there if we could see the new pastor. She told us he was not there. I asked where we could find him. She said,

"He didn't come to be our pastor. He is living out on the coast."

I was puzzled. I thought I had heard the Lord tell me to give the new pastor three hundred dollars. Confused, we drove back home with the money. Later, the Lord impressed us to send it to another pastor who needed help. We did. We obeyed the Lord. We gave the whole five hundred dollars away as He led us.

Six months later, a friend came to visit. In the conversation, the name was mentioned of the original pastor to whom we had tried to give the three hundred dollars. I asked the friend what had happened to that man. He told us that he did not take the pastorate of the Morton church because he had financial problems. He felt that if he became the pastor of the church, he would not be able to pay his debts. He had accumulated three hundred dollars of debt!

Just think about it. Where might that man be today if he had acted in faith? God had prearranged a miracle for him; his debts would have been paid, but unbelief held him back, and he missed a miracle. However, my faith continued to grow.

I am convinced that many of us have prearranged miracles waiting for us, but fear of the unknown causes us to miss them. Doubt is a thief. (Incidentally, within a year of that event, we had a new car!)

Never Act Out of Fear

When we believe God's Word, we won't respond to life's trials out of fear. The following parable that Jesus told about the kingdom of God reveals the Father's heart concerning money:

> "Again, it will be like a man going on a
> journey, who called his servants and entrusted

his property to them. To one he gave five talents of money, to another two talents, and to another one talent, each according to his ability. Then he went on his journey. The man who had received the five talents went at once and put his money to work and gained five more. So also, the one with the two talents gained two more. But the man who had received the one talent went off, dug a hole in the ground and hid his master's money.

"After a long time the master of those servants returned and settled accounts with them. The man who had received the five talents brought the other five. 'Master,' he said, 'you entrusted me with five talents. See, I have gained five more.'

"His master replied, 'Well done, good and faithful servant! You have been faithful with a few things; I will put you in charge of many things. Come and share your master's happiness!'

"The man with the two talents also came. 'Master,' he said, 'you entrusted me with two talents; see, I have gained two more.'

"His master replied, 'Well done, good and faithful servant! You have been faithful with a few things; I will put you in charge of many things. Come and share your master's happiness!'

"Then the man who had received the one talent came. 'Master,' he said, 'I knew that you are a hard man, harvesting where you have not sown and gathering where you have not scattered seed. So I was afraid and went out and hid your talent in the ground. See, here is what belongs to you.'

"His master replied, 'You wicked, lazy servant! So you knew that I harvest where I have not sown and gather where I have not scattered seed? Well then, you should have put my money on deposit with the bankers, so that when I returned I would have received it back with interest.

"'Take the talent from him and give it to the one who has the ten talents. For everyone who has will be given more, and he will have an abundance. Whoever does not have, even what he has will be taken from him. And throw that worthless servant outside, into the darkness, where there will be weeping and gnashing of teeth.'" (Matthew 25:14-30 NIV)

We will use God's resources wisely if *we know His heart*. By faith, we understand that God wants to bless us abundantly above all we ask or think. His heart shows us the purposes of His blessing, which is to reach those living in fear and without Jesus.

Active Faith Believes God's Word

Why all this emphasis on faith? Faith is the foundation of all that God wants to do for us. God's Word says that we cannot please Him without faith: "But without faith it is impossible to please him: for he that cometh to God must believe that he is, and that he is a rewarder of them that diligently seek him" (Hebrews 11:6). Therefore faith must be a priority issue in the life of the believer.

God also says that it only takes a very small amount of faith to accomplish big things. Jesus said, "If ye have faith as a grain of mustard seed, ye shall say unto this mountain, Remove hence to yonder place; and it shall remove; and nothing shall be impossible unto you" (Matthew 17:20).

What greater reward in life could there be than to find and develop faith in an almighty, all-powerful, loving God? The Bible puts great emphasis on faith. In the Gospels, Jesus was amazed at few things, yet He raved about the faith of many people He met. He said to one hopeless woman, sick for twelve years, "Your faith has saved you."[1] Regarding a nobleman of means, he said, "I have not found so great faith."[2]

On another occasion Jesus was asked by some of those who followed Him, "What shall we do, that we might work the works of God?" (John 6:28).

Did Jesus tell them to stop drinking, stop smoking, stop going to the movies, and go to church four times a week? No. Jesus answered, "*This* is the work of God, *that ye believe on him* whom he hath sent" (John 6:29, italics mine).

The Lord's answer was not performance. Not religious activity. Not following tradition to the letter. No. He simply wants us to believe. Our "work" is to have faith in God.

If you want to please God, simply believe Him. God's Word has much to say about believing Him.

I love the story in Acts 16 about the jailer who was in charge of keeping the apostle Paul and Silas in jail. Suddenly a great earthquake shook the foundations of the prison, opened the doors, and loosed all the prisoners. The keeper was about to kill himself, because he supposed that the prisoners had fled. But Paul stopped him, saying, "We are all here."

The jailer fell down before Paul and Silas and asked them to tell him what he had to do to be saved. Paul and Silas said simply, "Believe on the Lord Jesus Christ, and you will be saved, you and your household" (Acts 16:31 NKJV).

Paul wrote to the Romans, "If you confess with your mouth, 'Jesus is Lord,' and believe in your heart that God raised him from the dead, you will be saved" (Romans 10:9 NIV). Paul also wrote, "The just shall live by faith" (Romans 1:17). In Romans 3:20-22, he explained that we are made righteous by faith, not by deeds of the law. In essence, we are saved by faith, not by performance: "Being justified freely by his [God's] grace through the redemption that is in Christ Jesus" (Romans 3:24).

Paul also wrote, "For by grace are ye saved through faith; and that not of yourselves: it is the gift of God: not of works, lest any man should boast" (Ephesians 2:8-9). If we were saved by our performance, then we could boast. But we were saved through faith. Pondering these Scriptures will feed your faith and starve your doubt.

As we have seen, Paul focused on faith in the New Testament. In 1 Thessalonians 3, we see that Paul was not interested in the performance of the believers in the churches he had established. He didn't ask questions such as, "How many people were saved? How were the offerings? What was your attendance?" No. He was concerned about their personal faith; he wanted to revisit them to help where they were lacking in faith. Paul sent Timothy to strengthen their faith (see vv. 2-6), and he was happy when Timothy reported that their faith was strong.

The entire chapter of Hebrews 11 is about what faith is and about the great men and women whose lives testified of their faith in God. In that chapter, there are forty verses about faith. What a great emphasis on faith! The Word says, "For whatever is born of God overcomes the world; and this is the victory that has overcome the world—our faith" (1 John 5:4 NAS). Our faith is the victory that overcomes the world.

I have only shared a few verses on the subject of faith. I encourage you to spend time searching the Word for truth concerning this vital subject. Faith (believing) is a key to unlocking God's provision.

Feed your faith and starve doubt.

- Faith comes by hearing, and hearing, and hearing, and hearing!

- God is a faith God, and faith really pleases Him.

- Financial giving is evidence of faith.

- God looks for faith, not performance.

Chapter Six

Trust God and Enjoy His Best

God is good; He is a loving Father. He wants us to have the best. Yet we often doubt that fact. God gave me a great opportunity to prove that He wants good things for us when I was pastor of the church in Washington state.

We were driving the old Dodge I had bought while I was in college. I knew I should replace it. To my surprise one day, "out of the blue," I received a call from a car salesman in Seattle. His first words were, "Don, can you come up with a hundred dollars?"

"Why?" I asked.

"We have a brand new black Plymouth for you. If you bring in a hundred dollars, you can drive it away." He urged me to come to Seattle.

Marlene and I prayed. The offer sounded too good to be true; however as we prayed, we felt it was God's will. We could barely come up with a hundred dollars, but we decided to "go for it."

We drove to Seattle. That night I prayed again at our friend's house. I heard a clear word. "This is My will. Buy the car. Don't look at a used car." I *knew* it was God speaking.

The next morning we went to the dealership. The salesman took us to see the car. It was beautiful. I liked the shiny black color. So we agreed to buy it. He took us into his office and got the papers out. He started filling in all the details. Then, I asked how much the payments would be. His answer floored me. The monthly payments he quoted to me would be an amount equal to one-half of our income every month! My hands started to sweat. My heart began to pound. I wanted that car, but I felt it was impossible to make those payments.

The problem was, I knew it was God's will. I was in agony.

I failed the test. I finally stood up and rejected the deal. I tried to figure out how I could buy food, gasoline, and clothes for a baby and still make those payments. I was convinced that there was just no way we could afford that car. So I turned down the deal and walked out. I felt so discouraged because I had planned to drive a new car home.

We walked past a used car lot. I stopped and looked at a used Dodge. Not only did I look, I bought the car! I did the very thing I had heard the Lord say not to do. We drove home in a different car, but my joy was gone. My faith had wavered and failed. I felt like a whipped dog.

For weeks afterward I beat myself over the head, wondering why I had done such a stupid thing. How could I have failed to believe the Lord? I had no faith for months. I lost my anointing as a pastor. I wanted to quit the ministry. I was at the lowest level of discouragement. I knew I couldn't go on that way in the ministry. I had missed God's best. I finally repented and asked God to forgive me. I pleaded with the Lord to give me another chance to believe Him. I got peace, and the anointing returned.

That experience of failing to believe was one I have never forgotten. I have had many challenges of faith since, and I never want to go back into that awful feeling of discouragement again.

The key to this story is that *I knew* I heard the voice of God. I *knew* God told me not to buy the used car, but I disobeyed Him because I didn't have the faith to believe. *Faith and obedience always go together.*

I am convinced now that if I had stepped out in faith and bought that black Plymouth, we would have had increase in the church. My payments would have been covered, and I would have been "down the road" in a life of faith. I became determined to attain and maintain faith. I returned to the Word so my faith could be restored. These Scriptures built my faith:

> So Jesus answered and said to them, "Have faith in God. For assuredly, I say to you, whoever says to this mountain, 'Be removed and be cast into the sea,' and does not doubt in his heart, but believes that those things he says will come to pass, he will have whatever he says. Therefore I say to you, whatever things you ask when you pray, believe that you receive them, and you will have them." (Mark 11:22-24 NKJV)

> But without faith it is impossible to please Him: for he who comes to God must believe that He is, and that He is a rewarder of those who diligently seek Him. (Hebrews 11:6 NKJV)

> So then faith cometh by hearing, and hearing by the word of God. (Romans 10:17)

God expects us to have faith. The Bible says that we cannot please Him without it. If that is true, it is possible to get so full of God's Word that faith leaps in us! All of Satan's designs are thwarted through our faith in God.

The Word reveals the devil's strategies and teaches us how to take dominion over him. Through the Word of God, faith becomes so strong that fears, anxieties, tests, and problems have no effect on us. Faith is certain that God is good. Faith knows that all bad is from the devil. Faith knows that God plans only good for us.

As we believe God's Word, we find His plan. As we learn God's will, and do it, we enjoy it.

Meditate on God's Answers for Your Needs

Meditating on prosperity Scriptures will produce prosperity. Meditating on healing Scriptures will bring healing. Meditating on God's goodness will release His goodness into your life. As you study the Word, your faith will grow for your healing as well as for your prosperity. Meditate on God's Word so that when you speak, your words will be filled with His promises.

Joshua 1:8 NIV is full of promise for prosperity, saying: "Do not let this Book of the Law depart from your mouth; meditate on it day and night, so that you may be careful to do everything written in it. Then you will be prosperous and successful." Take time to think about that promise.

The Lord promises that we will be blessed if we meditate on His Word:

> Blessed is the man who walks not in the counsel of the ungodly, nor stands in the path of sinners, nor sits in the seat of the scornful; but his delight is in the law of the LORD, and in His law he meditates day and night. He shall be like a tree planted by the rivers of water, that brings forth its fruit in its season, whose leaf also shall not wither; and whatever he does shall prosper.(Psalm 1:1-3 NKJV)

The emphasis here is that we will prosper if we meditate on the Word of the Lord. It is so important to keep the Word in our inner man so that we can speak words of faith when we face trials (see Ephesians 3:16).

I see Christians suffering tremendous battles that could be resolved by faith. God's Word says that healing is God's will for the believer:

> God anointed Jesus of Nazareth with the Holy Ghost and with power: who went about doing good, and healing *all* that were oppressed of the devil; for God was with him. (Acts 10:38, italics mine)

> When the even was come, they brought unto him many that were possessed with devils: and he cast out the spirits with his word, and healed all that were sick: that it might be fulfilled which was spoken by Esaias the prophet, saying, Himself took our infirmities, and bare our sicknesses. (Matthew 8:16-17)

Why would God choose to make a believer sick? Remember, the Word declares that healing is always God's will. The Word of God also states that prosperity is always God's will. Would God choose to make people poor? No!

> Keep therefore the words of this covenant, and do them, that ye may prosper in all that ye do. (Deuteronomy 29:9)

> This book of the law shall not depart out of thy mouth; but thou shalt meditate therein day and night, that thou mayest observe to do

according to all that is written therein: for then thou shalt make thy way prosperous, and then thou shalt have good success. (Joshua 1:8)

Let them shout for joy, and be glad, that favour my righteous cause: yea, let them say continually, Let the LORD be magnified, which hath pleasure in the prosperity of his servant. (Psalm 35:27)

This next Scripture declares that God's promises are part of His blessings, and poverty is part of the curse. "Christ hath redeemed us from the curse of the law, being made a curse for us: for it is written, Cursed is every one that hangeth on a tree: that the blessing of Abraham might come on the Gentiles through Jesus Christ; that we might receive the promise of the Spirit through faith"(Galatians 3:13-14). We are heirs to the promise of Abraham. Why would we believe that God wants us to be poor and living in lack with shortages?

Faith Must Be in Your Heart and Mouth

Faith is stored in your heart and spoken through your mouth. Always keep the two working together. Believe with your heart, and say what you believe with your mouth.

Attain and retain faith in God by feeding on His Word continually. Faith will slip away if you don't keep refilling your mind with the Word. When your mind is full of God's Word, you will say, "The peace of God rules my heart" (see Colossians 3:15-16).

I am simply encouraging you to read the Word of God so you will trust in His goodness. Stop and think about what you are reading. Meditate on it. Look up the meanings of the words. Read commentaries on the passages you are reading. When you find something that speaks to your need, look for other Scriptures on that topic.

What consistently goes into the heart will eventually come out of the mouth. Meditation of God's Word will produce a good confession over your circumstances. Pray as the psalmist David did, "Let the words of my mouth, and the meditation of my heart, be acceptable in thy sight, O LORD, my strength, and my redeemer" (Psalm 19:14).

Meditating on what God has promised in His Word will change things in your life to conform to God's good plan for you. It will change your finances. It will change your marriage. It will change your physical well-being and your mental attitude. Reading the Word even ten minutes a day will bring change into your life.

If your heart is full of the Word, you will be able to ignore negative comments and negative influences that the devil uses against your prosperity. Jesus knew that God is good. *The Amplified Bible* says, *"Overhearing but ignoring what they said, Jesus said to the ruler of the synagogue, Do not be seized with alarm and struck with fear; only keep on believing!"* (Mark 5:36, italics mine). This means to consider and observe the Word of God, not your circumstances. "He that observeth the wind shall not sow; and he that regardeth the clouds shall not reap" (Ecclesiastes 11:4).

Retain faith by speaking God's promises with your mouth. Keep speaking the truth of His Word. *Boldly say what you believe.* Jesus did. He claimed to be the Son of God even though He was mocked for it. Abraham spoke of nonexistent things as though they existed. He gave thanks that he was the father of many nations even though he didn't have a son at the time the promise was made to him. Abraham's faith was in a good God, who calls those things which do not yet exist as though they did.[1]

In Proverbs 4:20-22 NKJV the Lord says, "My son, give attention to my words; incline your ear to my sayings. Do not let them depart from your eyes; keep them in the midst of your heart; *for they are life to those who find them, and health to all their flesh*" (italics mine).

The Hebrew word for *health* in Proverbs 4:22 literally means a medicine, or a cure; figuratively deliverance.[2] I can testify that my wife and I have studied and meditated on the Word of God for fifty years, and we have had good health all these years. The Word of God is a good medicine for us.

When Satan comes with doubt, just proclaim, "God fights for me because I keep His Word in my heart! God's will is for me to prosper, and I am prospering in Jesus' name!" This is not engaging in mind over matter. This is activating a positive confidence in the Word of God.

Use your faith every day or it will shrink. Never give in to what you see or feel. Don't waver. Hold fast to your confession of faith in God's Word (see Hebrews 4:14; 10:23). Next, I will show you the great reward that is promised to those who trust God to give them His best. But first remember key #6.

Trust God to give you His best.

⛏ Never doubt God's goodness.

⛏ Just reading is not meditating—meditating takes time and concentration.

⛏ Faith is expressed by your words, so watch your mouth.

⛏ To do the works of God—believe!

Chapter Seven

Obey and Watch for Miracles

One of the most profound tests of my life came in 1970 when I almost lost everything. It was a traumatic year: I had built two nursing homes, one in California and one in Washington state. Two in one year was extraordinary. This involved providing more than 265 beds and spending two million dollars. It also required tremendous amounts of cash flow of which I had no concept at that time.

I had a desire to expand my business. A Christian friend from California introduced me to financiers in his area. They were fast-talking salesmen. They made great promises to finance several facilities for us. With their expertise, they said they could find eight million dollars to build four new nursing homes. I felt uneasy with their fantastic promises and schemes, but we needed money so we proceeded with these men, not realizing how ungodly they were.

They finally had financing processed to the point where the bank accepted the loans, and these men received their fees and disappeared. Construction began in Port Orchard, Washington. Then suddenly everything fell apart. My first loan didn't come through after all. It was a mess. Worse than that, in the meantime, my competitor had started construction on a similar facility next door.

There was a reason for this trouble: I had not taken time to be sure of God's will before getting involved with those men. When everything was going wrong, we realized we needed to pray and find God's will.

We halted all activity on the project. I knew if I stopped, we would lose more than $50,000. But that would be better than losing a million dollars. Marlene and I waited on the Lord for two weeks. We had to know what to do. (Fortunately, we *can* know God's will.)

Two weeks later, we knew we should go ahead with the project in Washington state. The Lord confirmed it in several ways. From the book of Job we read, "So the LORD blessed the latter end of Job more than his beginning" (Job 42:12). I knew we would be blessed with more. Also, my two administrators, Gene Asa and Sam Sutherland, agreed that we should go ahead, and we all had peace to move on with our plans.

We were able to get other financing. This new financing was a miracle as well. Once a loan has fallen through, it is not easy to borrow money again. Then my attorney learned of an insurance company in Denver, Colorado, that might lend us the money.

We flew to Denver and met with the president of the company. We went to lunch, and as the food was served, I asked to give thanks to the Lord for the meal. He dropped his fork and said, "Okay." At that meeting, we got the money we needed. I was so happy.

Interestingly, my attorney later shared with me what had influenced this man to lend us the money. He had told my attorney that he was impressed when I prayed over the food. He thought if I was bold enough to do that, I must have principles and the kind of character that he could trust.

As a result of this miracle, we built the buildings. But then we had to fill the empty beds. We held an open house and started accepting residents. The day we opened the new facility, we had an unusual experience. That same day, two fine-looking gentlemen walked in and explained that they had a need for beds to house rehabilitation patients. They asked if they could rent 26 of our 119 beds. In a few months, they asked for another 26 beds. We were half full!

Amazingly, this facility, which had seemed so illogical to build, became the quickest success of any nursing home I had built. It became profitable sooner than any other home we had opened.

However, the financial testing had just begun. We were to experience a real financial crunch. It was during this time of pressure that I was forced to make a decision that would stand me in good stead the rest of my life.

When we opened the new facility, finances were extremely tight (partially due to the fact that we opened a new facility in California at the same time). Soon the mortgage payments were due. We had very little income because too many of the beds were empty for the first few months. It was a great test of faith.

When the payroll came due, I wondered where we would get the money to meet it. Fear crept into my thoughts. I didn't know how we would pay for the food to feed our residents.

On top of all this, we had financed the equipment and furniture separately. It had been delivered and was in our buildings. We owed $250,000 on it, and we didn't have the money to pay for it. When creditors began demanding payment, it was embarrassing to tell them we had no money. We kept stalling, looking for funds. I was desperate.

In the middle of all this stress, my good friend John Osteen called one day and said, "I want you to go with me to Africa." He and I had traveled overseas many times ministering to people. I thought, *Go to Africa now? You've got to be kidding.*

I wanted to go, but I didn't have the money. The business had me under great pressure. I told John I couldn't go because of the financial burden.

Several days later, I was confronted with the gnawing question, "Are material things more important to you than spiritual things? Is money more important than helping people?"

I remembered the Bible admonition, "But seek ye first the kingdom of God, and his righteousness; and all these things shall be added unto you" (Matthew 6:33).

Again, I reaffirmed a very important principle in my life: Spiritual matters must take precedence over material things. I determined that I would not be ruled by logic, but by a personal relationship with Jesus Christ and His Word. I decided that faith would rule my life, not circumstances or logic. I stood firm on the conviction that "ministry comes first; money will follow."

I traveled with John Osteen to Kenya, to South Africa, and to the Congo. We had great ministry times of encouraging missionaries and helping to build their faith. I had put "first things first." I had obeyed God.

After this decision to obey God, *no matter what the cost*, and always put Him first, we received a new loan. Everything worked out. I know now it was because I had put God's will in first place.

Note this interesting fact: That year, 1970, was the hardest year financially in our whole lives. Yet that year we gave $17,000 to the Lord's work!

Obedience Is Better Than Sacrifice

Through His prophet, God told King Saul, "To obey is better than sacrifice" (1 Samuel 15:22). I had proven that fact.

Too often *obedience* is a word we don't want to hear. We have a tendency to accept or reject some portions of Scripture that require obedience on our part; I call that "selective obedience." We want to choose which commands we will obey.

Then we "shove aside" other portions with excuses like, "That doesn't apply to me," or "I can't do that; it's too hard," or "I'll do that later." If we become selective in obeying parts of the Word of God, we will limit the blessing of God in our lives. We will miss great anointing because of disobedience. We will miss His best for us.

The decision to obey God no matter what the cost established an important core value in my life. It has stayed with me all these years. It has brought exceptional success in my life. I learned to put God first in all the affairs of life.

Putting God first may seem very difficult. Perhaps you fear that God will ask too much of you. You may think you will end up with shortages in your finances. Many Christians have developed the fear that if they get too close to God and start obeying Him, they will end up poor. They think that poverty and spirituality are somehow linked together. But I have not found this poverty concept to be true.

There is no virtue in poverty. In fact, the opposite is true. God has good things planned for us. He desires that we be generous, just as He is. As we obey Him, He surprises us with benefits we had not planned. He did that for me.

The life of faith and giving is usually just acting on the Word of God as the Holy Spirit leads us. It is generally contrary to logic or to circumstances. Often the Lord will lead us to give money to individuals or missionary work at a tremendous stretch of faith on our part.

I have experienced financial miracles by giving to missions. As a result, God has turned my negative approach into a positive one. He showed me that I can give material things and also be blessed with material things.

Actually, God puts all of us to the test sometimes. He may ask us to give an amount that seems totally unreal. We may say, "That's too much. That's too far out of my comfort level. No way." But, if we pass the test and give what He puts in our heart to give, then His blessings will come to us.

Patience is part of passing the test. Once we obey God, most of us want the blessing immediately. Learn to be still, and wait. In fact, give the Lord thanks, because He won't fail. Let God bless you in His way and in His time. He *will* do so!

My heart has always been in support of missions. I am a man with a world vision; as I have noted, I have been in sixty-nine countries. I often went to Mexico to be with missionary Danny Ost. In Mexico City, he had built two large churches, which he called centers, each seating two to three thousand people. He worked so hard, but hundreds were saved each week—not monthly, but *weekly*.

One day he came to Seattle saying God had put it on his heart to build another center in Mexico City. It was to be next to a bus depot where thousands of people passed daily. He said it would take more than $400,000 to build. The next thing I knew, I was hearing the Lord say, "Give $50,000!" It was mind-boggling! I was already tithing and giving. It seemed impossible.

However, I knew it was God, and so I told Danny what I would give. I gave about half of it right away. Then, each week or two, I sent more toward my commitment.

One morning as I was shaving, I started thinking of the need in Mexico and of my promise to help meet that need. But I had no more money. I had given every dollar I could scrape up from every business we owned.

I looked in the mirror and said, "God, I'm sorry, but I just haven't been able to give the whole $50,000. I want to, but I just can't."

I heard the Lord say, "Who gave you the figure that you were to give?"

I said, "You did."

He said, "Then why do you stop believing Me now?"

I asked forgiveness and said I would believe to finish it.

I kept giving, and in just a few more weeks, I had given the full amount. It is hard to explain how it happened, but God provided.

I was excited when it was all given. It was a great feeling to know I had stretched my faith and had fully obeyed the Lord.

Be Trustworthy with Your Money

Hoarding money is destructive. It is evidence of selfishness and unbelief. Money becomes our god if we can't give it to others when God tells us to do so. If we refuse to tithe (allot the first 10 percent to God), it is a sign that we don't know Him or that we don't trust Him.

To be successful in business, to help others, and to give into God's kingdom we need strong faith in God and His Word. We need money and wisdom—and both come from God.

God must be able to trust us with money. We must be careful about the use of funds that God puts into our hands.

When I was ready to graduate from college, spring came, and I had not paid my tuition. I had been pleading, "Please God, supply my need for tuition!" To my surprise, one day I received enough money to pay it off—but then I used the money for something else!

I needed a car. I had been taking the bus to school or riding with other students. Now I had some money, so I went looking at cars. (I shouldn't have.) I knew I would need a car when school was out and I had graduated. So what did I do? I took the money the Lord had given me to pay my tuition and bought a black, shiny Dodge. It was great to have my own car.

Then the end of the school year came. The college demanded my tuition, telling me that I would not graduate or receive a diploma until I paid my bill.

Again, I cried out to God. "Lord, what will I do?" For several days, I continued begging the Lord to help me financially.

Then in a quiet moment, I heard His small inner voice say, "I gave you the money for tuition, and you used it for something else. I answered your prayer, and you violated My provision."

I felt ashamed. I knew I was guilty. I asked the Lord to forgive me and agreed with Him that I would never do that again.

That lesson has stayed with me all of my life. When God provides for a specific need, that money must be used for that specific answer. We must not expect God to meet our needs, then use His provision on selfish, materialistic satisfaction of carnal desires. God will come through for us if we show Him we can be trusted.

Sacrificial Giving Is Faith in Action

In 1963, we were new in business. One of our nursing homes was losing money every month. It was a huge four-story, 140-bed facility. The problem was we had twenty empty beds. We were "in the red" with debt exceeding our income month after month. Sometimes I had to borrow from other accounts to cover payroll for that facility. I knew that situation could not go on forever.

One day Marlene said to me, "Donald, we should give to the Lord from this facility."

"How can we give from a business that is in the red?" I exploded. I tried to tell her that she didn't understand business. I scolded her, "How can we give when we don't make any money?"

She insisted that we should honor the Lord anyway. A few weeks later, the Lord told me to give a thousand dollars to our church from that facility. I told Marlene what God had said, and she agreed immediately, without even saying, "I told you so!"

Now, I am the "great man of faith," but my thinking was, *Okay I'll give the thousand dollars. At least the Lord will get it before we go bankrupt!* Regardless of my doubt, we obeyed and gave.

We must honor God, obey Him, and let Him prepare the results. That is what He did. Within ninety days, all the empty beds were filled, and the facility was in the black financially.

We hired a new administrator, Harold Becker who discovered errors that were causing profit losses. He found private patients in rooms with four beds. He found welfare patients in private rooms. The laundry was pouring too much chlorine in the water and eating up the sheets. He made the necessary adjustments, and we started to make a profit again.

All this changed when we released that thousand dollars. We were thrilled, and our faith grew. Then I was excited about doing even more for the kingdom of God. I learned that obeying God's direction to give always brought reward. In the next chapter, we will look at the basics of giving a tithe of all our income to the Lord's work.

Expect miracles when you obey God.

- Focus on a relationship with Jesus, not on material things.

- Don't be "selective" in your obedience to God.

- Hoarding money is selfish and limits the flow of financial blessing.

- Release for increase!

Chapter Eight

Give 10 Percent—It's Not a Tax!

P aying 10 percent of your income to God is tithing. You don't have to do it; God is not charging you a tax, but experience quickly taught Marlene and me that our tithe was a good investment. We had been married nearly two years, and I was still the pastor in the church in Washington, when I first learned this truth.

The Lord led us into a new ministry that required more traveling, and after six months a difficult situation arose. We had no meetings for about two months, so our income was almost nothing. Finances were so tight that we had to use every cent just to eat and pay for gasoline to travel. During those two months I didn't tithe. I felt I couldn't.

We were invited to lead meetings at a church in Garibaldi, Oregon. I had a small trailer house, which we hooked up and drove through Portland on our way to Garibaldi. We had gotten into heavy traffic, and I turned a corner too sharply. The trailer house caught the front of another car and ripped a gaping three-foot hole in the side of our trailer. I was sick with worry. I wondered, *Why this?*

I was under even more pressure after this accident because we had no money. We finally arrived at the church. That Saturday night I was whining to God, "Why did all this happen when I am out serving You?"

As I kept praying, the Lord spoke clearly in my heart, reminding me that I had withheld our tithes. This act had opened the door for the devourer, to cause trouble and destroy our fruit. It was so real to me that I quickly repented and asked forgiveness. I promised the Lord that I would pay the back tithes and not do that again.

When we held meetings in those days, churches normally took up an offering for the evangelist after the week of meetings had ended. But this pastor took one for me the first Sunday night, and I was able to tithe and give immediately.

But, I still had a hole in the side of my trailer. After the two weeks of meetings were over, we returned to my folks' house where we were staying. A friend in the ministry, David Grant, said he and his father could repair the hole. They did, and the trailer looked like new. It didn't cost me a cent. We were praising God for His faithfulness, even though I had been disobedient.

What a powerful, but stressful, lesson I had learned. Holding back the tithe is based on unbelief. We can't hold back the tithe (the seed) and expect God's fullest protection and provision. It just won't work. We can't eat the seed out of fear and then expect to get a harvest when no seed is planted.

We must put our faith in the fact that God provides both the seed that we need for sowing and the increase of our harvest as the Word promises:

> And God is able to make all grace abound toward you, that you, always having all sufficiency in all things, may have an abundance for every good work.
>
> As it is written: "He has dispersed abroad, he has given to the poor; his righteousness endures forever."
>
> Now may He who supplies seed to the sower, and bread for food, supply and multiply the seed you have sown and increase the fruits

of your righteousness, while you are enriched in everything for all liberality, which causes thanksgiving through us to God. (2 Corinthians 9:8-11 NKJV)

As we tithe and give joyfully, God has delight in showing us how He keeps His Word. The Bible clearly states:

"Bring all the tithes into the storehouse, that there may be food in My house, and try Me now in this," says the LORD of hosts, "If I will not open for you the windows of heaven and pour out for you such blessing that there will not be room enough to receive it. And I will rebuke the devourer for your sakes, so that he will not destroy the fruit of your ground, nor shall the vine fail to bear fruit for you in the field," says the LORD of hosts. (Malachi 3:10-11 NKJV)

It is possible that you struggle, as I did, with the thought of having 10 percent less money than you do now if you tithe. You may already be facing many unexpected expenses each month. You may wonder, *How can I tithe and still meet my expenses?*

But as a young man in Oregon, I withheld tithes and learned an expensive lesson the hard way. Not tithing was a *big* mistake!

Tithing Really Pays!

We proved that tithing protects us from the devourer in a very practical way through our California facility, which we call the "Redding miracle."

In 1970, we built a 165-bed convalescent home in Redding, California. We established a procedure for all of our administrators to send a tithe to be put into the work of the Lord from each month's business income. We have done this for more than forty years.

At the time of construction, we had to install seventy-five air conditioners in the facility because of the very hot summers. A few months after we opened the nursing home, I found that the manufacturer's manual indicated the air conditioners would last seven to eight years. It was disturbing to think that in eight years I would have to replace all of the cooling systems.

I told our administrator, Harold Becker, to keep records on the units. I wanted to know how long they lasted.

Twenty years later I asked Harold how many of the air conditioners he had replaced. He said, "Five." Thank God, seventy of the air conditioners had lasted twenty years!

When I told that story, someone said to us, "Boy, are you lucky."

It had nothing to do with luck, but everything to do with God's promises and our obeying Him with our tithe. God kept His Word from Malachi 3:11: He rebuked the devourer for our sakes so that Satan could not destroy the fruits of our ground. Wear and tear, rust and corrosion are devourers. God gave us a miracle. He saved us thousands of dollars in replacement costs.

God cannot, and will not, violate His promises. His timing may confuse us, but He cannot fail. The miracle at the Redding facility proved that God's economic system is higher, better, and more successful than the world's system.

Considering wear and tear on equipment, I am reminded of another special experience in Fall City, Washington, where we lived for twenty-two years. We had dug a well on the property down to about 250 feet. The pump in that well had served us for twenty years, then it died.

I called a man to come and replace it. When he pulled the pump out, he asked how long it had been down there. I told him it had been pumping for twenty years. He reacted, "No way. These pumps never last over ten years." I reassured him I was telling the truth.

He just shook his head and said, "You are sure lucky."

After he had installed the new pump, I realized once again that the pump's long life was the result of our tithing. God had done His part in minimizing the wear and tear on our pump. He had rebuked the devourer—wear and tear on the pump. Thank You, Lord!

When you tithe, God will rebuke the devourer on your behalf. God says, "That man is a tither, leave him alone, Satan. Keep your hands off his money." God will protect you from the devourer, just as He did with our pump and air conditioners.

God's Superior Economic System

The Bible is full of keys to God's economic system. One of these keys is in the book of Malachi, the last book of the Old Testament. I have shared portions of it earlier, but I want to comment on the entire passage, before sharing more of my personal testimony.

> "Will a man rob God? Yet you have robbed Me! But you say, 'In what way have we robbed You?' In tithes and offerings. *You are cursed with a curse, for you have robbed Me, even this whole nation.* Bring all the tithes into the storehouse, that there may be food in My house, and try Me now in this," says the LORD of hosts, "If I will not open for you the windows of heaven and pour out for you such blessing that there

will not be room enough to receive it. And I will rebuke the devourer for your sakes, so that he will not destroy the fruit of your ground, nor shall the vine fail to bear fruit for you in the field," says the LORD of hosts; "And all nations will call you blessed, for you will be a delightful land," says the LORD of hosts. (Malachi 3:8-12 NKJV, italics mine)

This is a shocking Scripture. Who wants to be under the curse of God? Not me! God has no desire to see us under a curse. His desire is that we be under His blessing and protection, not a curse.

However, there is a condition in this Scripture. His promises accompany conditions; He will do His part *if* we do ours. God pleads with us to tithe and give offerings.

We give 10 percent of our income to the Lord, and then we have 100 percent of the remaining 90 percent to spend to meet our obligations and to give to others. The more we give from that 100 percent (of the 90 percent), the more we will have coming back in return.

Some statistical studies reveal that less than 20 percent of Christians tithe, so that means that 80 percent of believers don't tithe. If believers don't tithe, God calls them thieves in Malachi 3 because they are robbing Him of the firstfruits of what He has given them (see Proverbs 3:9 NKJV). This may sound harsh, but you may be sitting next to a thief every time you go to church! *I am* not calling anyone a thief; God is.

Just imagine what the church could do if every believer tithed and gave offerings. We would make an impact in the world and make Jesus known everywhere on this globe.

We Christians may quote Philippians 4:19 and loudly proclaim, "God will supply all my needs." But He won't if we don't obey Him. Remember, every promise has a condition. We can quote promise after promise, again and again, but if we don't obey and give, those promises won't be fulfilled.

Investments Earn Good Returns

I am reminded of the story of a postman who noticed a certain old man who came and opened his mailbox every day.

Finally, the postman asked the man, "Are you looking for something special?"

"Yes," the white-haired man replied, "I'm waiting for a check in the mail."

"Great," the postman said.

The old man continued to come, day after day. Several days went by and the postman again asked, "No check yet?"

"Nope," said the man, "but I believe I'll get it."

Finally, after many more days, the postman got up the nerve to ask, "Who are you expecting the check from?"

The man explained that he was expecting money from General Motors because he had heard it paid good dividends.

The postman responded, "So you bought General Motors stock, eh?"

The old man said, "No, but I believe I receive."

We know that if there is no investment, there are no dividends. When we obey God by investing our tithes and offerings, we will see money coming our way. It will come in unusual ways from unexpected sources.

Some people give impressive donations to charitable organizations, but this giving is not the tithe. Some give money to relatives in need or to TV evangelists, which is good, but that is not God's instructions for the tithe. *The tithe belongs to the house of God.*

God's storehouse is where you get your ongoing spiritual food. You wouldn't receive a meal at one restaurant and then go pay for it at another one. In the same way, your tithe belongs to your local church, where you get fed spiritual food.

Perhaps another book should be written about the importance of each believer belonging to a local church where he or she can receive a steady diet of God's anointed Word through a pastor. The Bible clearly tells us in Hebrews 10:24-25 that we are to "consider one another in order to stir up love and good works, *not forsaking the assembling of ourselves together,* as is the manner of some, but *exhorting one another,* and so much the more as you see the Day approaching" (Hebrews 10:24-25 NKJV, italics mine).

In that verse, *consider* means "behold, . . . discover, perceive."[1] We are to consider each other so that we can exhort each other and stir up good works in each other. There are many other Scriptures that teach the importance of the body of Christ working together corporately as we share our spiritual gifts to keep each other walking in faith. Our tithes should go to that storehouse where we share in corporate worship and work with other believers.

In America, there is no excuse for people to claim they can't find a local church so they must give their tithes and offerings someplace else. The tithe doesn't belong in parachurch groups or media ministries. Offerings (above the tithe) can go to radio and TV ministries that contribute to our lives, but they are not God's storehouse where our firstfruits tithe belongs.

The fact is that you don't have to tithe, but if you don't, God is not obligated to bless you with more than you can use. In fact, if He did so, He would be a liar. But if you do tithe, God has said that He will "open the windows of heaven for you and pour you out a blessing, that there shall not be room enough to receive it" (Malachi 3:10 AMP).

God said to put Him to the test concerning this issue of tithing. What a statement! You can test God. Tithe and give offerings, and He will open His resources of abundance to you. He says He will *pour out* abundance, not just sprinkle a little. He will open the windows *of heaven*, not the windows of earth. He will pour out *more* than you can contain, not just enough to get you by.

But there is a condition attached to this promise. The condition is this: obey by tithing and giving. Just do it and see God prove His Word to you! If you don't tithe, if you don't give offerings, you are under the curse of the devourer. That is a terrible place to be.

Who wants to be under a curse? Not me! By tithing and giving we keep the curse off of ourselves.

If we want God to "come through" for us, then we must do what He tells us to do. He will not violate His word. My son, Dan, shares the following story of how he realized this truth:

Dan's Testimonial

Growing up in a home where giving was a way of life one would think it would be easy to go out on one's own and continue as one had been taught. I found it was easy to watch someone else be a giver, but when it came my turn, it was easier said than done.

As I moved away from home and joined the working crowd, I would look at my income and think, *How can I tithe, much less give?* So I struggled with this for many years.

Then I came to a realization that my way wasn't working. I watched people around me becoming more successful and not just in finances but also in every area of their lives. I became a bit jealous, but in a motivating way.

I realized that giving equals receiving; God set this simple equation in motion from the beginning of time. The equation is not to give so you will receive, but to give to help others and further God's kingdom and let God's equation work on its own. I made a decision to say yes and no to God's equation.

I said yes to committing to a lifestyle of giving. Once that decision was made, I had to say no every time the thought came that I couldn't afford to give because of the way my finances looked. I had to stick to the commitment I had made to give.

Making the right choices in life are sometimes the harder choices, but they have the greater rewards.

So anyway, years ago, I made a decision to change my thinking and to change my attitude as well. I started to give a little more than I thought I could. And what do you know!

Life started to change. New friendships began to develop, the atmosphere at home was more relaxed and peaceful, and my financial situation started to improve. As a testimony to the financial side of things, my business has had a steady annual growth of 20 percent per year! That's a hundredfold every five years!

Needless to say, giving has become fun and rewarding. When there's a need, or when we just feel prompted to give, we follow the leading and enjoy it. There's no place on earth where you can invest like this and the return is so great!

A Special Tithe

About two years after we returned from the Philippines, we bought fifty-two acres of beautiful land in Fall City, Washington, about thirty miles east of Seattle. We built a home there, having sold our house in Seattle. The cost of this attractive, three-thousand-square-foot ranch-style home was about $55,000. (Imagine that!) We lived there for twenty-two years, and enjoyed many happy events with our boys and entertaining family and friends.

After twenty-two years, we sold the house for $175,000. I was happy because we were building a new home in Bellevue, Washington. One afternoon, as I was thinking about how nice it was to make such a good profit, the Lord reminded me that we needed to tithe on the increase.

I knew that the Word said, "Honour the LORD with thy substance, and with the firstfruits of all thine increase: so shall thy barns be filled with plenty, and thy presses shall burst out with new wine" (Proverbs 3:9-10). But now we were looking at a tithe from $120,000!

A tithe on that amount shocked me. I struggled with it for a few days, but finally realized that we could not lose if we obeyed the Scriptures. My natural mind told me that we needed that money for our new house, but commitment to the Lord's will was more important. We obeyed, and it released miracles for us later in our lives.

Reasoning can cause us to miss God's will and His good plan for our lives. It can also block prearranged financial miracles He has planned for us. Tithing is not just 10 percent of salary. Tithing must be from all increase in income.

When pastors teach on tithing and giving, some religious people are offended. I know people who have said, "If I had a million dollars, I'd give half of it to the Lord." The problem is that they don't have a million dollars; but since they don't give half of the five hundred dollars they do have, their claim is doubtful. Pastors should not be intimidated when they hear people complain that they talk too much about money. The only way to build faith for finances is to teach and teach and teach.

People who are not excited about giving, and who react negatively to this message of blessing and protection, probably struggle with this concept of tithing. But, I believe they will have many wonderful experiences ahead as they take this step of faith and begin to tithe. We can't start giving "big" until we start giving "small."

God isn't looking for wealthy people to bless; He is looking for obedient people through whom He can demonstrate His power.

It is time for us believers to be the example of what God will do for those who obey Him. We should be the blessed ones. We should be the envy of sinners. We should do well and prosper. When we tithe and give, God keeps His Word. He gets the glory. It is not what we did, but what He did. Giving 10 percent is just the beginning of seeing God's abundance in our life. In the next chapter, we will look at how much God loves a cheerful giver.

Invest 10 percent of your income in God's work.

🔑 Maintain God's blessing and protection by tithing; God will deliver you from the devourer as you tithe.

🔑 Give 10 percent of your income as a tithe to your local church, the place where you are spiritually fed.

Chapter Nine

Guarantee Prosperity—Be Generous

Giving generously is like throwing a boomerang. But in God's economy, if you throw one boomerang many will come back to you. Whatever you give, more comes back to you. The Word promises, "A generous man will himself be blessed, for he shares his food with the poor" (Proverbs 22:9 NIV). It is the same with giving of yourself, your time, your talents, or your money. The more you give, the more others give to you.

For the purposes of this chapter, I refer to *giving* as money given *above the tithe to the Lord*. The Word teaches in Leviticus 27:30 that the tithe doesn't belong to us, it belongs to the Lord. As the tithe belongs to the Lord, we can't say, "I'm giving," when we are paying our tithes. *Giving* is the amount given beyond the Lord's portion.

Dare to Give Beyond Reason

When we talk about "giving," we tend to think of giving to the church or some charitable organization. However, Jesus said, "Give, and it shall be given to you." He didn't say to whom. Just give. Again, I had direction from the Lord to give, not to the church but to our employees.

As we tithed and gave offerings from the business each month, our business prospered. One year, I was talking to the staff at our facility in Port Orchard, Washington. I was telling them that we give to charitable work. I was honoring God by sharing His blessing on the business income.

A few days later one of the nurses commented to our facility administrator that it was nice to give to God, but how about giving more to the employees? When the suggestion was passed on to me, it hit me hard.

We always tithe. We give to the Lord's work. But, give generously to employees?

As I thought about the nurse's comment, the Lord spoke to me. He reminded me that He had been good to me, and now He impressed me to bless the employees. "Share the profits with the employees," I heard Him say, "Give a large salary increase to your employees."

For two days I pondered the consequence of giving raises to my employees. I looked at the financial statements and decided it was a big stretch of the imagination to take this step. But, I finally determined to do what God said.

I said to the Lord, "Okay, how about a 10 percent raise?"

His answer was overwhelming. The Lord said, "Increase salaries by 50 percent." I couldn't believe it. Impossible! My first thought was, *God, You don't understand!*

Yet I knew this instruction was from the Lord. I certainly would not have initiated this huge financial increase on my own. I also knew that the devil *never* tells me to give.

To increase the salaries of my employees by 50 percent would be a giant step of faith! But faith pleases God.[1] The Word also says, "He that hath pity upon the poor lendeth unto the LORD; and that which he hath given will he pay him again" (Proverbs 19:17). Even though our employees were being paid what other facilities paid employees in their positions, I realized that many of our nurse aides were poor and had to work extra just to make ends meet.

At the next managers' meeting I told them what God had challenged me to do. When I said we would increase salaries by 50 percent, they were shocked. They were punching on calculators and forcefully sharing that it was financially impossible. It would be a disaster.

I told them, "We will do this even if it means that I make no profit next year." I said, "We will take a step of faith, and we will help the poor. The Bible says that he who helps the poor lends to the Lord, and so God will repay us."

All my staff administrators are born-again Christians. They finally agreed, "It's impossible, but we'll believe with you and do it."(It's great to have such leadership.)

When we gave that salary increase to the employees they all clapped. (Partly in unbelief, I think.)

The end of the story is that when the financial statements came in for the next twelve months, we made the same amount of profit we had the year before. Yet, we had given many thousands to our employees.

Our giving defied logic. I couldn't reason it out. We can't allow reason to rule our actions. Reason is often Satan's tool to keep us from acting in faith and enjoying the miracles God has for us.

To show how God worked in that situation, I will explain how some of the increase came. Three months after I increased salaries by 50 percent, the state of Washington established a new system of pay for welfare residents. They said they would reimburse the nursing homes on the basis of their costs. We had to give the state officials our financial statements listing all expenses. When they received our figures, they noticed that our payroll costs were high because of our salary increases that year.

When my two nursing homes in Washington received their newly established rates, we had one of the highest rates in the state. Because of my payroll, I was reimbursed on a higher basis. Praise the Lord! This was another *big* miracle for us.

Later, a fellow nursing home owner asked me, "Ostrom, I notice that you have one of the highest rates in the state. How did you get it?"

I answered in smugness, "I had inside information."

When you give of your money, you are doing what God commanded. You are fulfilling a scriptural principle: "Give and it shall be given to you" (Luke 6:38). Every time you fulfill a Scripture, you need not worry about the blessings coming. They will come.

Giving is a sign of unselfishness. Generous giving is strong evidence of faith in God and His Word.

God Said, "Let Go of the Van!"

God's Word says in Proverbs 11:24-25 NIV, "One man gives freely, yet gains even more; another withholds unduly, but comes to poverty. A generous man will prosper; he who refreshes others will himself be refreshed."

Marlene and I drive nice sedan cars, but we can't load firewood or haul huge boxes in them. I couldn't take the Mercedes to the mountains and sleep in it overnight. I wanted a van. I watched for the right one. I found some that were very attractive. But I felt impressed by the Lord that the van I wanted would be in the south side of Seattle. So I waited.

Sure enough, months later I found the perfect Dodge van. It had all-leather upholstery, electric seats that became a bed, TV, air conditioning, and much more. I knew this was the one the Lord had saved for me. It was so fancy for most families that the dealer couldn't sell it. I received a good price because the dealer was happy to finally get rid of it.

I loved that van. I went to the mountains, stayed in campgrounds, and roamed the trails in that van. I could go to the lake and stay a couple of nights in my van stocked with food and goodies. It was fun. I loved it. I did that for about a year and a half. It had low mileage and was in excellent condition.

Then one day, out of the blue, I heard the Lord say to me, "Let go of the van. Give it to a man of God."

I knew about whom the Lord was speaking.

"Oh, no, Lord. You gave this van to *me*. I need it."

"Need it?"

Well not exactly. But this time obedience was a tough decision. This beautiful, two-tone, flashy van was my pride and joy. I considered how I had willingly let a few others use it. *But why would I have to give away my van?*

Beware of Greed

Many years ago the Lord impressed me not to hold to material things too tightly. If He wants our "stuff," and we won't let go, then we can be sure that greed has set in.

Beware of greed. It can creep in without your knowing it. Greed will limit what God wants to do for you.

I had a choice in this matter, and I finally gave that van joyfully to a thriving ministry where thousands of men were being saved every year. I felt an "umbilical cord" attachment to that ministry after that. It made me happy to be a part of what they were accomplishing, and I knew I would share in the rewards.

It was also wonderful to realize that I was not bound by material possessions. I was free and could enjoy God's presence without guilt, and without putting limits on His provision.

Not all giving requires a great test of faith. Sometimes we have funds to help others but are just not listening to the

Spirit when He wants us to help someone else. Timing may be a very important part of being a good and faithful servant.

I am reminded of another experience I had while on vacation in which simple obedience turned around a minister's life. We were at Lake Chelan with our family one summer. We happened to see Rev. Gwyn Vaughn, an evangelist friend, at the park where we were staying. We visited for a while and then went back to our motor home.

I was only there for a few minutes when I heard the Holy Spirit say to me, "Go back and give the evangelist a hundred dollars."

I didn't wait. I wrote a check and took it to Gwyn immediately. He thanked me profusely, and they left the next day. About two years later, he told me his story. At the time I gave him the check they had no money for gasoline or food. He was totally discouraged and ready to quit the ministry. But when I obeyed God, giving him the hundred dollars, it caused him to realize that God had not forgotten him. Since that time, he and his wife have had many years of satisfying and productive ministry together. One little gift, one small obedient step, and a ministry was saved!

Be obedient and faithful as God directs. Never limit your expectations of what God can do with your willingness to serve Him. He can multiply the fruit of your obedience many times beyond what you can imagine.

Key #9

Give generously to guarantee prosperity.

☞ Remember the boomerang principle—the more you give, the more comes back to you.

☞ Overrule logic when challenged to give; sometimes God is not logical.

☞ Giving is evidence of unselfishness.

☞ Givers love the offering time!

Millionaire Faith Key

113

Chapter Ten

Push the Envelope—Defy Logic

To experience generous giving, we must pursue a *bold, aggressive faith* that defies logic and obeys God. I am not talking about a passive, weak, wimpy faith. Bold faith is the determination that God will give us what He has promised.

We must make up our mind that we will not be denied. Aggressive faith is that bulldog kind of faith that hangs on and won't let go. Aggressive faith believes God for the supernatural, and it includes an attitude that claims, "As a child of God, I have the right to all the promises given to me in the Bible."

There is a challenge here, however. Faith often— almost always—reaches beyond common sense. At the same time, common sense is valuable and necessary in life. However, we must learn to recognize God's unlimited ability to go beyond common sense. To have the faith to believe, we *must* understand in our hearts the power of this fact: God is *not* limited.

You may wonder how you can begin to grasp such a concept; it defies understanding. However, this is the key. Get out of the mental realm. Stop trying to figure out everything in the natural mind. Faith is of the Spirit, and it defies logic.

The Mind of Faith

We must start thinking the way God thinks. *His way of thinking is clearly revealed in the Bible.*

What defines our thinking process? Is it the news media's negative view? Is it our family situation? Is it financial problems? Does fear for our job, nagging sickness, or unrest in our church shape our thinking?

Faith comes by renewing the mind (see Romans 12:2). How do we do that? We start by thinking as God thinks.

God's thinking process is revealed in His Word. As you study and meditate on the Word continually, it will begin to define and shape the way you think. Through it, He will renew your mind. The faith to be a giver will become a part of your thinking as you renew your mind in the Word of God.

Continue to read the Word, or your resolve to obey God will begin to be replaced by the patterns of this world. Renewing your mind is a daily, life-giving habit, and with it comes faith—often without your even noticing.

Your friends may not understand the changes you are making in your life. They may even criticize you. Circumstances may seem to contradict what God is promising you, but have faith in Him.

Jesus had to ignore what other people said. *The Amplified Bible* says, "Overhearing *but ignoring* what they said, Jesus said to the ruler of the synagogue, *Do not be seized with alarm and struck with fear; only keep on believing*" (Mark 5:36, italics mine). Don't let yourself be ruled by circumstances. Be ruled by God's promises and by the faith that He will keep His Word.

You must continue to believe no matter what the world tries to tell you is reality. Refuse doubt. Feed your faith, starve your doubts, and learn to defy logic if faith tells you to do something beyond your understanding.

The Bible says, "He who observes the wind will not sow, and he who regards the clouds will not reap" (Ecclesiastes 11:4 NKJV). In other words, pay attention to what you are doing. Consider and observe the Word of God. You must not let circumstances rule your decisions and actions.

God Prospers Those Who Give

One year God challenged us to bless the employees again. The Lord made it clear that we should provide funds for a retirement benefit for the people who worked for us. At that time we had about five hundred employees, so we had to designate a large amount of money each year or it wouldn't mean much for each participant.

We took another step of faith and determined to give $50,000 a year into the program. We deposited the funds. The very next quarter we experienced the best quarter in our business until that time!

The challenge is to obey God, to step out in faith. When we do, He creates unusual events and circumstances to honor us.

This is probably a good place to share with you some Scriptures that God made real to me regarding helping our employees. These Scriptures are faith-builders for all who want God to promote them to a position of leadership. These principles guide relationships between employers and employees.

> Look! The wages you failed to pay the workmen who mowed your fields are crying out against you. The cries of the harvesters have reached the ears of the Lord Almighty. (James 5:4 NIV)

He who oppresses the poor to increase his wealth and he who gives gifts to the rich—both come to poverty. (Proverbs 22:16 NIV)

He that hath pity upon the poor lendeth unto the LORD; and that which he hath given will he pay him again. (Proverbs 19:17)

He who gives to the poor will lack nothing, but he who closes his eyes to them receives many curses. (Proverbs 28:27 NIV)

For the worker deserves his wages. (Luke 10:7 NIV)

To increase salaries 50 percent was a big step of faith. It was beyond my logic. As a businessman, it just wouldn't "pencil out." But faith pleases God.

Do you want God to trust you with more money? Then give money away. Give to the poor. Give generously every time God tells you to do so. Give to the church. Give to missions. Give generously. There will be no lack or shortage because you keep giving money away.

It will hinder our financial success if we hoard our money.

The Lord warns us of the danger of greed and covetousness in Luke 12:15 NIV, saying, "Watch out! Be on your guard against all kinds of greed; a man's life does not consist in the abundance of his possessions."

When we keep on giving, we keep ourselves free from the spirit of greed. In 1 Timothy 6 NIV, we are warned about the love of money. Verse 10 says, "For the love of money is a root of all kinds of evil. Some people, eager for money, have wandered from the faith and pierced themselves with many griefs."

Most of us now agree that *money* is not the root of evil. It is the *love of* money that gets us in trouble. I have taught around the world that there is one way to know whether we have the *love of money*. I repeat it here: If we won't tithe and give offerings, the love of money has trapped us.

Anyone on the road to becoming a Christian millionaire will always be a generous giver. I know many Christian millionaires, and every one of them is a liberal giver to the poor, to God, and to the church.

Why be a generous giver? Remember the Scripture, "Give, and it shall be given unto you; good measure, pressed down, and shaken together, and running over, shall men give into your bosom. For with the same measure that ye mete withal it shall be measured to you again" (Luke 6:38).

The key here is that the "same measure" that you use to give to others will be used to "measure" to you. *If you give generously, you will receive generously.*

Give money to those in need, and contrary to logic, it will come back to you. *Beware of logic!* Remember, "He who has pity on the poor lends to the LORD; and he will pay back what he has given" (Proverbs 19:17 NKJV).

God Said, "Send Money to Your Friend"

One year my wife and I were on vacation in Hawaii. I was by the swimming pool when a friend of mine, Ron Devore, came to my mind. Ron is now a missionary in Africa, but at that time he had a youth center where he was helping kids leave their rough lives and follow God.

There by the pool I heard the Lord say to me, "As soon as you get home, send $1,200 to Ron."

I was surprised at this directive, but I decided I would do it—if I remembered it.

When I got home, the Lord reminded me again. So I called Ron and told him what the Lord had said. I told him I would have the $1,200 in the mail the next day. Ron was astounded. He told me that the rent was overdue for the youth center he was operating—in the amount of $1,200!

Ron was thrilled that I obeyed God, and so was I. My own faith was strengthened to know that the Holy Spirit can speak to us and use us if we are careful to listen to Him, any time or anywhere. I learned from the urgency of Ron's situation that quick obedience is very important. Delay could be disastrous.

Tithing and Giving

Tithing is not giving. Giving is beyond the tithe. Remember, our tithe belongs to the Lord; it is not ours to use. I learned to tithe as a teenager. But I didn't have abundance until I started giving beyond my tithe—out of the other 90 percent.

You may feel that you are giving when you tithe. However, the Bible says that the tithe is the Lord's: "A tithe of everything from the land, whether grain from the soil or fruit from the trees, *belongs to the* LORD; it is holy to the LORD" (Leviticus 27:30 NIV, italics mine). We are not really *giving* when we tithe; we are simply releasing to God what belongs to Him.

The remaining 90 percent is ours. We are stewards of that money. When I started to give out of the 90 percent, I began to see increase. I started having "more than enough." I began to have surplus to help others.

When I came into the ownership of the business, and I realized that I should tithe from all my facilities, I immediately thought it would be impossible.

What is impossible with men is possible with God (see Luke 18:27). Remember these three words: abundance, surplus, and increase (see Matthew 13:12, Malachi 3:10, and Proverbs 3:9-10). These words describe God's attitude toward financial provision. God wants us to have more than enough. We should be able to help others with our abundance.

The Word says, "Let him that stole steal no more: but rather let him labour, working with his hands the thing which is good, that he may have to give to him that needeth" (Ephesians 4:28).

We don't experience abundance, surplus, or increase until we give out of the 90 percent that is ours. Start giving beyond the tithe and start seeing surplus, good deals, and "lucky" breaks.

My children have put these principles into practice and have prospered continuously. I remember when our youngest son, Paul, and his wife were struggling financially. At that time they were invited to a fund-raising banquet for a missionary. I saw them raise their hands to give. I didn't know that they gave five hundred dollars! I gasped when I heard it, thinking they couldn't afford that amount.

However, when they gave, it released God to do a miracle for them. Soon afterward a neighbor offered them enough paint to paint their entire house. The money they saved was far more than the amount they gave. God keeps His Word: "Give, and it shall be given unto you" (Luke 6:38).

The Higher Economic Principles of God's Word

The challenge is to get out of our intellectual approach to God and into the higher economic principles of His Word.
Imagine giving money away so you can have more! How foolish to eat into your income when you need it to pay bills and feed the kids.

God's higher economics are found in His Word: "One man gives freely, yet gains even more; another withholds unduly, but comes to poverty. A generous man will prosper; he who refreshes others will himself be refreshed" (Proverbs 11:24-25 NIV).

The apostle Paul wrote, "In everything I did, I showed you that by this kind of hard work we must help the weak, remembering the words the Lord Jesus Himself said: 'It is more blessed to give than to receive'" (Acts 20:35 NIV).

Malachi 3:8-11 speaks of tithes *and offerings*—not just tithes. When we start giving out of our 90 percent, we see the devourer destroyed. The "devourer" is rust, wear and tear, wind, fire, etc. When we give, we start seeing miracles.

Remember these promises:

> Whoever sows sparingly will also reap sparingly, and whoever sows generously will also reap generously. Each man should give what he has decided in his heart to give, not reluctantly or under compulsion, for God loves a cheerful giver. (2 Corinthians 9:6-7 NIV)

> No servant can serve two masters: for either he will hate the one, and love the other; or else he will hold to the one, and despise the other. Ye cannot serve God and mammon. (Luke 16:13)

The love of mammon (or riches) is the work of an evil spiritual power that grips and enslaves people through love of money. It is the lust for money that is never satisfied. But it is very difficult for greed to destroy the person who tithes and gives generously. Be a generous giver and watch God's blessings pour into your life.

Defy logic and push the envelope.

- Bold faith defies common sense.

- Renew your mind with the Word of God to develop faith.

- Ignore criticism of your bold faith. Don't let others define faith for you.

- God entrusts money to those who are generous givers.

Chapter Eleven

Protect Your Integrity—Secure Success

Never be afraid to be honest. Don't be afraid that you will lose money or position because you demonstrate the godly character of integrity. God will honor you and promote you. The testimony of a Christian friend of mine, George Reece, illustrates this truth.

George started his career of building homes as a young man. He operated his own construction business for several years, and then a large firm hired him. Because he was faithful and hard working, he received several promotions.

One day, George was asked to meet with the two senior partners of the company. They took him for coffee and sat in a secluded area of the restaurant and started asking him questions about his work and job. Finally, one of them leaned forward and asked, "George, if it was necessary, for the good of the company, would you lie for us?"

George's thoughts raced: *Here goes my job. Here goes my career.* He waited before answering. Should he lie? He knew it might be the only way to keep his job.

However, that still, small voice deep down inside said, "You can't lie. You are a Christian." After a long pause, George took courage and spoke clearly and confidently, "No, I cannot lie for you." He waited for the expected termination.

The senior partner leaned back, gave a sigh of relief, and said, "Good. Now we know we can trust you. With that answer, we have another question, how about becoming a partner in the business?"

George was overwhelmed and excited. He stayed true to his convictions. Even though he thought it would bring negative results, he did not compromise. As a result, the Lord favored him, and he was promoted. He is a man of principle and of godly character. God honored George in his position. Today, George is a wealthy businessman. God can trust him. God can place millions of dollars in his hands.

Character Is More Important Than Ability

True success is the result of quality of character and nobility of spirit. To neglect the spiritual life and not develop godly character is to invite defeat. At the least, this neglect will minimize any level of success.

The business leader who focuses on and develops quality of character will gain the confidence and respect of his community. Strength of character is all-important. Integrity is the key to a good reputation. It speaks of reliability and trustworthiness. It produces trust.

What is character? One dictionary says it is moral firmness or vigor; especially acquired through discipline. It also speaks of behavior, habits, and competency. For me, character has to do with honesty, integrity, and moral purity. Character requires personal respect and respect for others. We can't have strong faith if we lie to people. We can't have dynamic faith if we cheat others out of money.

I had the opportunity to prove the quality of my character many years ago. Our facility in Bremerton, Washington, was an old hospital building that we constantly updated for fire regulations. One year, we had to put in fire doors and smoke detectors. We chose a neighbor of mine to do the work since he owned an electrical business. We agreed upon a price for the total job and put it in writing. We agreed the work was to be finished within ninety days.

After sixty days of working on the building, the contractor said he needed more money. We fussed, but finally gave him more. The ninety-day period ended, but the work was not finished. Worse yet, he needed more money, a lot more.

We said no, and demanded he finish the job. He explained that he was losing a lot of money because of the old building construction, but we held firm. He finally completed the work, but feelings were not good between us.

One day the Lord said, "Pay him for the extra time and expense."

I argued, "Why? He doesn't deserve it. He didn't keep his word. He caused us problems." But I couldn't get away from God's instruction. I knew I should obey God and pay the man the extra money.

When I called my administrator and told him to send the money, he was shocked. "No way," he said. "That guy has caused me lots of grief." I said, "I know that, but pay him anyway." He mailed the money, and I felt relieved and free.

Then shocking news came. Two weeks after we paid my neighbor the "undeserved" money, he died! How glad I was that I had obeyed God. I had no guilt on my conscience.

In my business, people know we don't lie. They know we have moral standards. We pay our bills. We keep our word. We don't cheat. We are fair. We are reliable. As a result, people recommend our facilities to their friends. So do the doctors.

We have a high percentage of occupancy in our convalescent homes. Why? I can't put an ad in the newspaper saying, "Are you about ready to die? Come and see us." No, we depend on referrals from families of previous patients. Our reputation leads people to come to our business. The integrity of our character creates confidence in the quality of care we give.

Quality Care in Our Business

As I have explained, my business is caring for the elderly. We have skilled-care facilities, apartments for the elderly, and assisted-living facilities. We have been in business for more than forty years. Competition has become a big issue, especially since there are big national companies who have hundreds of millions of dollars to invest in marketing their services.

Yet, we have survived in style. How? Let me share the principles of our success.

Our primary interest is giving quality care to our residents. A secondary goal is to maintain a great atmosphere in each facility. One way to do that is to hire the best employees and pay them well. Our third interest is making a profit.

Many years ago, a CPA told us that we could make much more profit than we do—and many other facilities like ours were making more profit. We were told that we hired too many nurses, and that we should terminate some. Financially, the "bottom line" would look better.

That must have been the procedure of many of our competitors. But, my primary concern is the care of the residents. To cut hours of care meant inferior care. I refused to do that. Another suggestion was to terminate the long-term employees and hire new people at smaller wages. Save money! I refused that concept too.

I took the attitude that God would supply what I needed. I determined to believe God to protect my business. I decided that quality care was absolutely essential. I would be loyal to and appreciative of longer-term employees. Yes, it did cost more money, but I asked the Lord to bless the business so we could do it.

Here is the history of our industry. In the last few years, three of the larger companies in our field of nursing care have gone into bankruptcy. Their main concern was the "bottom line," financial only. The result was poor care, which resulted in a bad reputation, which resulted in empty beds.

Conversely, we focused on excellent care. The cost was more, but the atmosphere in our facilities was different. Our staff was happy. They worked efficiently without so much grumbling. Our reputation was excellent. The result, even doctors would recommend our facilities. Because of our good reputation, our beds were full. And because of that, we have had a good margin of profit.

I believe it all had to do with my motives and my faith in God to supply the need for the standard of excellence. God honored my faith. We honored Him with our integrity and our tithes to the Lord. Putting faith in God first makes good business sense.

We have long-term employees who are happy with our standards and goals of quality care. I have had two administrators work for me for thirty-two years. Another man worked with us for twenty-eight years. We have many employees who have worked with us for twenty to twenty-five years.

By the way, if we were to operate out of fear, the temptation would be to terminate the longtime employees and hire new ones at much less cost. I have never followed that course. I believe God to pay my employees well, regardless of longevity. God has always honored that attitude in my company.

Godly Character Requires Humility

Character is linked with humility. Genuine humility inspires trust. The Bible says "with humility comes wisdom" (Proverbs 11:2 NIV). Humility and wisdom instill confidence. Like God, we are drawn to a humble person, but repulsed by the proud (see James 4:6 and 1 Peter 5:5). A false humility will eventually be recognized as "fake" and produce distrust.

How foolish to think we are so capable and smart that we don't need the help of others—or of God. Pride is a natural weakness of every one of us. The serious danger of pride is that we don't know we have it until something drastic happens.

The Word of God declares, "By humility and the fear of the LORD are riches and honor and life" (Proverbs 22:4 NKJV). The proud person has the attitude: "*I* can *make* this work. *I* can handle this by myself. *I* have the brains and the ability." The humble person knows he needs God's help. He depends on wisdom from God to hold up a standard of excellence and succeed in accordance with godly principles.

In the business world, seemingly insignificant character traits make a *big* difference in a person's success. For instance, answering a letter or phone call in a timely manner demonstrates good character. When information is requested, a person with good character will answer as soon as possible.

Even if he or she doesn't have the answer, a person with high moral excellence will call and say so. He or she will not keep people guessing about a decision or plans.

Another excellent character trait that brings godly success is demonstrated by keeping our word. When a commitment or appointment is made, we must keep it, and be on time. If we don't, we impose our schedule on others. They lose time because of our failure to be punctual. We should respect the time another person has allotted to us.

How frustrating it is if we block out time for someone, but they don't show up for the meeting. We lose valuable time that could have been given to others. The same is true when we fail to keep our appointments on time; we waste other people's valuable time, and we destroy our own reputation for honesty and reliability.

The key to integrity is self-discipline. The issue is honesty. A person's reputation can be unjustly destroyed, but not his character. Development of character and maintaining humility are basic keys to keeping a good reputation. In these modern times, the world looks for talent and ability, but God looks for character. God will bless and honor the one who develops godly fundamentals in his or her life.

When a person doesn't keep his word, and fails to do so often, he loses credibility—and eventually his reputation. When a man stretches the truth, sooner or later it catches up to him, and he loses business. A businessman who is deceitful and who promises a product or delivery when he knows he can't produce it will soon lose his reputation.

There is something delightful about working in the business world with leaders who have convictions and moral purity. It is also a noticeable quality when a new acquaintance states he doesn't drink; that speaks of moral conviction. But if an associate flirts with the girls, tells off-color jokes, talks about X-rated movies, refers to adult Internet sites, or brags about "conquests" of women, it reveals his own moral weakness.

If he takes a pen or pencil that doesn't belong to him, his action says he is dishonest. If he speaks well of his church, but criticizes his pastor, he reveals his true lack of integrity.

Godly success begins with godly character. Character starts with the spiritual condition of the person. The closer we are to God, the better our moral values, and the better our moral values, the more God will honor our obedience.

Unforgiveness Is a Destructive Characteristic

Many years ago, I learned the graphic lesson that harboring unforgiveness stops the flow of God's blessings. I lost thousands of dollars, not knowing that my bitterness was the cause.

I had a close friend whom I had helped to become successful in winning others to Christ. We had worked together for years, going overseas to help reach people with the gospel.

In the course of events, he was accused of wrongdoing, things I knew he would not do. I defended him. As time progressed, certain men treated him with dishonor, and I built up a bad attitude toward them. I criticized them and talked about them to others. My attitude became so bad that I didn't want to see them at meetings. I avoided them.

It was really none of my business, but I took offense for my brother. I wanted to defend him, to protect him, but inadvertently I became secretly bitter toward his accusers. I harbored unforgiveness in my heart toward them. Criticism invaded every area of my life. Soon, I was criticizing my wife, my pastor, my employees, and my friends.

One day, unexpectedly, I heard the Lord say to me, "Ask forgiveness of those men for your attitude."

"No way!" I responded. "They should be coming to me asking forgiveness." I was stubborn and refused to obey the Lord.

The very next day, a friend from another country sat beside me and said that he had noticed that I had changed from my usual happy self. He said that something "not so good" was coming out of my life.

He caught me totally by surprise when he said to me, "Don, I think you should go to those brothers and ask forgiveness for your attitude."

It was like a knife going through me. Here was a friend telling me the same thing the Lord had spoken. It was too much! I knew the Lord was being patient and gracious to get me to repent. I knew I had to obey if I wanted God's blessing on my life.

I called the leader of the group and asked to meet with him. We did meet, and I asked him to forgive me. I told him I would fly to the board meeting and ask all of those men for forgiveness. He accepted my apology and said he would relay it to the others.

I felt good as I left the room. Now I could face these men without fear or disgust. As I walked to my room, I heard the Lord say, "Now your beds will fill at the nursing home in Bremerton." I was shocked! What did those twenty empty beds have to do with my asking forgiveness? I couldn't believe there was any connection.

We had been struggling financially for several months. I had been rebuking the devil, and calling those beds full, but nothing was happening.

Two days later, I called Sam, our administrator in Bremerton, and asked him how things were going. He said, "Don, we've started taking residents again."

I asked, "When did that start?"

He said, "Two days ago."

Within two months our facility was full.

We had lost about $60,000 that year. It was a very expensive problem. I learned the lesson, however, that unforgiveness and bitterness can block the blessing and protection of the Lord in our lives.

We must maintain godly character and be quick to forgive. We must not harbor resentment. We must let it go. The sooner we do, the better.

Avoid Carelessness and Mistakes

I have learned to mix faith with everything I do. Faith is necessary for success. I learned to reject the idea, or lie, that I had no faith. I learned to refuse the thought that I would never be strong in faith. In fact, I determined to be a man of strong faith. I have focused on the power of faith and the power of our words.

By now, after all of these stories of great encounters with God's miraculous provision, I may have left the impression that I never have problems or tests anymore. But Satan is not asleep. He paces and prowls "as a roaring lion . . . seeking whom he may devour" (1 Peter 5:8). He will attack in any area to keep us from enjoying the benefits and blessings of God.

However, our problems are often caused not by the devil, but by carelessness on our part. We become the problem through wrong decisions and fleshly actions.

Maintain integrity in your life. Make this paraphrased Scripture from Psalm 18:20-23, and 25:21 your daily prayer:

Lord, reward me according to my righteousness (my conscious integrity and sincerity with You); recompense me according to the cleanness of my hands. Help me to keep Your ways and not depart from my God. Help me to keep all of Your ordinances before me, and keep me upright and blameless before You, ever on guard to keep myself free from my sin and guilt. Let integrity and uprightness preserve me, for I wait for and expect You.

Key #11

Guarantee success through integrity.

⚷ God protects an honest man and gives him favor.

⚷ Character is more important than talent or ability.

⚷ Honesty is not the best policy—it is the only policy for success.

⚷ People are more important than money.

⚷ God exalts the humble, but despises pride.

⚷ Be more concerned about your character than your reputation.

⚷ Bitterness and unforgiveness is a killer of the soul.

Chapter Twelve

Guard Godly Character

I have found nine characteristics that limit a person's quality of success in life. Of course, there may be more, but in this chapter I will share distinct attitudes to avoid, and the principle key to a godly character that will unlock prosperity in both your personal and business relationships.

Avoid Unbelief, Weak Faith, and Natural Logic

Unbelief always looks at the negative instead of the positive. If our minds are not saturated with the Word of God, our faith will be weak. Fear will creep in, and fear blocks miracles. We tend to reason with our carnal, natural minds and question God's ability to perform miracles on our behalf. Unbelief tends to limit our thinking (and God) to our own budget or salary. Faith looks beyond logic because often what God does is not logical.

God's response is:

> So then faith cometh by hearing, and hearing by the word of God. (Romans 10:17)

> But without faith it is impossible to please him: for he that cometh to God must believe that he is, and that he is a rewarder of them that diligently seek him. (Hebrews 11:6)

Now when he [Jesus] had left speaking, he said unto Simon, Launch out into the deep, and let down your nets for a draught.

And Simon answering said unto him, Master, we have toiled all the night, and have taken nothing: nevertheless at thy word I will let down the net. And when they had this done, they inclosed a great multitude of fishes: and their net brake. (Luke 5:4-6)

Avoid Criticism, Slander, and Gossip

A judgmental attitude and speaking against another person are two of Satan's greatest tools to steal our blessings. Criticism interrupts and defeats faith. Slander often results in our own poor health or financial difficulties. Gossip gives the devil a foothold in our lives. Criticism, slander, and gossip lead to our own poverty, sickness, depression, and discouragement. God's response is:

Do not speak evil of one another, brethren. He who speaks evil of a brother and judges his brother, speaks evil of the law and judges the law. But if you judge the law, you are not a doer of the law but a judge. There is one Lawgiver, who is able to save and to destroy. Who are you to judge another? (James 4:11-12 NKJV)

Remind them to be subject to rulers and authorities, to obey, to be ready for every good work, to speak evil of no one, to be peaceable, gentle, showing all humility to all men. (Titus 3:1-2 NKJV)

Judge not, that ye be not judged. (Matthew 7:1)

Avoid Sin, Disobedience, Indulgence, and Rebellion

Moses asked God's people, "Why are you disobeying the LORD'S command? This will not succeed!" (Numbers 14:41 NIV).

God paid an extreme price of Christ's blood, which was shed in pain and death, for our redemption. We fall subject to guilt, judgment, and condemnation when we disobey God. Separated from God's reaffirming love, we will suffer a needless and constant "put-down" of self.

When we rebel against God, and indulge in our own way, we cannot rise in faith because we become aware of our weaknesses. Through deliberate and intentional sin, we deny God the privilege of blessing us because He will not violate His Word. He must chasten us.

When He does correct us, we can quickly acknowledge sin, repent, and return to His blessings. God's Word says, "He who covers his sins will not prosper, but whoever confesses and forsakes them will have mercy" (Proverbs 28:13 NKJV).

God's response is:

But as he which hath called you is holy, so be ye holy in all manner of conversation; because it is written, Be ye holy; for I am holy. (1 Peter 1:15-16)

By humility and the fear of the LORD are riches and honor and life. (Proverbs 22:4 NKJV)

Our response should be:

I will set nothing wicked before my eyes. (Psalm 101:3 NKJV)

Avoid Pride and Insubordination

In pride, we tend to take matters into our own hands when we can't see what God is doing. Pride loves the praise of men. We step out of God's blessings when we are more concerned about pleasing people and making a good impression on them than we are with pleasing God. Pride is the essence of sin, and God hates it. He resists and opposes it, and He frustrates those who are proud.

God's response:

> Pride goeth before destruction, and an haughty spirit before a fall. (Proverbs 16:18)

> When pride comes, then comes shame; but with the humble is wisdom. (Proverbs 11:2 NKJV)

> For this is what the high and lofty One says—he who lives forever, whose name is holy: "I live in a high and holy place, but also with him who is contrite and lowly in spirit, to revive the spirit of the lowly and to revive the heart of the contrite." (Isaiah 57:15 NIV)

> The fear of the LORD is the instruction of wisdom; and before honour is humility. (Proverbs 15:33)

> But He gives more grace. Therefore He says: "God resists the proud, but gives grace to the humble." (James 4:6 NKJV)

Clothe (apron) yourselves, all of you, with humility [as the garb of a servant, so that its covering cannot possibly be stripped from you, with freedom from pride and arrogance] toward one another. For God sets Himself against the proud (the insolent, the overbearing, the disdainful, the presumptuous, the boastful)— [and He opposes, frustrates, and defeats them], but gives grace (favor, blessing) to the humble. Therefore humble yourselves [demote, lower yourselves in your own estimation] under the mighty hand of God, that in due time He may exalt you. (1 Peter 5:5-6 AMP)

Avoid Unwillingness to Tithe and Give

Refusal to tithe is real evidence of a lack of trust in God. The tithe belongs to the Lord, and God cannot bless a thief. When we withhold the tithe, we tie His hands to bless us. Eventually even poor health is connected to a refusal to tithe (which is stealing from God), because we have financial problems and start worrying. Worry leads to headaches, back problems, nervousness, mental attacks, and sleeplessness. God's response (we have looked at these verses before, but I list them again to establish their truth):

Give, and [gifts] will be given to you; good measure, pressed down, shaken together, and running over, will they pour into [the pouch formed by] the bosom [of your robe and used as a bag]. For with the measure you deal out [with the measure you use when you confer benefits on others], it will be measured back to you. (Luke 6:38 AMP)

Will a man rob or defraud God? Yet you rob and defraud Me. But you say, In what way do we rob or defraud You? [You have withheld your] tithes and offerings. You are cursed with the curse, for you are robbing Me, even this whole nation. Bring all the tithes (the whole tenth of your income) into the storehouse, that there may be food in My house, and prove Me now by it, says the Lord of hosts, if I will not open the windows of heaven for you and pour you out a blessing, that there shall not be room enough to receive it. And I will rebuke the devourer [insects and plagues] for your sakes and he shall not destroy the fruits of your ground, neither shall your vine drop its fruit before the time in the field, says the Lord of hosts. (Malachi 3:8-11 AMP)

One man gives freely, yet gains even more; another withholds unduly, but comes to poverty. A generous man will prosper; he who refreshes others will himself be refreshed. (Proverbs 11:24-25 NIV)

Avoid Bitterness, Resentment, and Anger

Bitterness is a destructive behavior because it questions the goodness of God. Resentment compares our circumstances with that of others and then says that God isn't fair. Resentment wonders, *Why are others blessed, and I'm not?* Resentfulness leads us away from blessings. Anger toward people is often evidence of anger toward God.

Questions rise in angry hearts, *Why? Why?* But when this happens, it is easy to become sarcastic and disrespectful and lose our peace. Beware the danger of self-pity. No matter how people treat you, don't feel sorry for yourself. Refuse to be hurt by people. Walk in love and respect for others.

Often confusion is the result of bitterness. Bitterness leads to sarcasm and contempt. Bitterness, anger, and resentment can produce physical ailments, even resulting in ulcers and stomach disorders. These ungodly characteristics interrupt faith and give the devil a foothold in many areas.

God's response:

> And whenever you stand praying, if you have anything against anyone, forgive him and let it drop (leave it, let it go), in order that your Father Who is in heaven may also forgive you your [own] failings and shortcomings and let them drop. *But if you do not forgive, neither will your Father in heaven forgive your failings and shortcomings.* (Mark 11:25-26 AMP)

> For if ye forgive men their trespasses, your heavenly Father will also forgive you: but if ye forgive not men their trespasses, neither will your Father forgive your trespasses. (Matthew 6:14-15)

> Let all bitterness, and wrath, and anger, and clamour, and evil speaking, be put away from you, with all malice: and be ye kind one to another, tenderhearted, forgiving one another, even as God for Christ's sake hath forgiven you. (Ephesians 4:31-32)

Avoid Strife with Your Spouse

God says our prayers are hindered when we are not in harmony and unity with our spouse (see 1 Peter 3:7).

Disrespect and criticism of our spouse only dissipate God's anointing on our lives. We can't fight in the home and still enjoy the blessing that God intends for us. Remember that much discord in a marriage involves money. No spouse should spend any sizeable amount of money without the agreement of the other. Too many times, knowledge "after the fact" creates anger or disappointment. Communicate. Trust each other.

God's response:

> Likewise, ye wives, be in subjection to your own husbands; that, if any obey not the word, they also may without the word be won by the conversation of the wives . . . Likewise, ye husbands, dwell with them according to knowledge, giving honour unto the wife, as unto the weaker vessel, and as being heirs together of the grace of life; that your prayers be not hindered. Finally, be ye all of one mind, having compassion one of another, love as brethren, be pitiful, be courteous: not rendering evil for evil, or railing for railing: but contrariwise blessing; knowing that ye are thereunto called, that ye should inherit a blessing. (1 Peter 3:1,7-9)

> The wife's body does not belong to her alone but also to her husband. In the same way, the husband's body does not belong to him alone but also to his wife. Do not deprive each other except by mutual consent and for a time, so that you may devote yourselves to prayer. Then come together again so that Satan will not tempt you because of your lack of self-control. (1 Corinthians 7:4-5 NIV)

Avoid Foolish Spending and Greediness

Lack of wisdom in purchases and overuse of credit cards gets us into trouble because we buy everything our eyes see. Then it is hard to recover. God calls that greediness and covetousness. Lack of discipline is the issue. Lack of self-control in the area of spending can bring financial stress, which creates fear, worry, and anxiety.

I am reminded of a young man I had counseled in business. He began moving in faith, and his business exploded in eighteen months. Cash became plentiful. What did he do? He bought a new Porsche and a house, and soon when business lagged, he couldn't keep afloat financially; he couldn't pay his bills, so he lost the business. Greed is a subtle thing.

God's response:

> And He said to them, "Take heed and beware of covetousness, for one's life does not consist in the abundance of the things he possesses."(Luke 12:15 NKJV)

> He that is faithful in that which is least is faithful also in much: and he that is unjust in the least is unjust also in much. If therefore ye have not been faithful in the unrighteous mammon, who will commit to your trust the true riches? (Luke 16:10-11)

> "And he said to him, 'Well done, good servant; because you were faithful in a very little, have authority over ten cities.'" (Luke 19:17 NKJV)

Avoid Negative Talk and Negative Attitudes

Constant murmuring and complaining can kill faith and give Satan a "foot in the door." We must not talk the problem. Instead, we should think on the promises in the Bible. We can control our thoughts and think on the good.

Guard your thoughts and the words you speak. Talk the promises; memorize them. See the good in others. Be an encourager. Speak faith and positive words.

God's response:

"For by your words you will be justified, and by your words you will be condemned." (Matthew 12:37 NKJV)

Death and life are in the power of the tongue: and they that love it shall eat the fruit thereof. (Proverbs 18:21)

A man shall be satisfied with good by the fruit of his mouth: and the recompence of a man's hands shall be rendered unto him . . . There is that speaketh like the piercings of a sword: but the tongue of the wise is health. (Proverbs 12:14,18)

A man shall eat well by the fruit of his mouth, but the soul of the unfaithful feeds on violence. He who guards his mouth preserves his life, but he who opens wide his lips shall have destruction. (Proverbs 13:2-3 NKJV)

Whoever guards his mouth and tongue keeps his soul from troubles. (Proverbs 21:23 NKJV)

For verily I say unto you, That whosoever shall say unto this mountain, Be thou removed, and be thou cast into the sea; and shall not doubt in his heart, but shall believe that those things which he saith shall come to pass; he shall have whatsoever he saith. (Mark 11:23)

I just listed nine hindrances to true success. Now let's look at a vital principle that offsets the hindrances I just mentioned and releases true prosperity into our life.

Adapt Praise as Your Language of Faith

Praise is a key to blessing and success. God said, "He who sacrifices thank offerings honors me, and he prepares the way so that I may show him the salvation of God" (Psalm 50:23 NIV).

We honor the Lord by praising Him. Furthermore, praise opens the way for God to work on our behalf. The more we give thanks and praise to God, the more He is released to answer our prayers.

God responds aggressively to a grateful heart. Consider this great and positive statement: "Sacrifice thank offerings to God, fulfill your vows to the Most High, and call upon me in the day of trouble; I will deliver you, and you will honor me" (Psalm 50:14-15 NIV).

Activate this great principle of praise: "Through Jesus, therefore, let us continually offer to God a sacrifice of praise— the fruit of lips that confess his name. And do not forget to do good and to share with others, for with such sacrifices God is pleased" (Hebrews 13:15-16 NIV).

The psalmist David said, "Enter into his gates with thanksgiving, and into his courts with praise: be thankful unto him, and bless his name" (Psalm 100:4).

Do it. Give God praise. Be thankful. Bless His name. Do good and share with others, and watch what happens. Expect divine intervention in your circumstances.

You will experience what King Jehoshaphat experienced. Several enemy armies joined to destroy Jehoshaphat and his people. Then he sent "praisers" out before the army. As they gave thanks to the Lord and began to praise Him, God intervened, and the enemy armies began to attack each other and defeated themselves (see 2 Chronicles 2:20). Praise is a mighty key to deliverance and victory in life.

Our God is a God of miracles. There is no limitation with Him! All things are possible. Believe and receive. God is good!

You can be an ordinary businessperson sitting in the pew with millionaire faith. You can know with certainty that God wants to prosper you for a purpose. He wants to bless you so that you can release funds to support and build His kingdom. Obedience to God's Word will cause financial blessings to flow through your life to help others and spread the gospel. It will give you purpose and joy unspeakable. Act in faith today, and expect God to prosper you for His purpose.

Be a person of godly character.

🔑 Resist unbelief, which looks at conditions and sees the negative.

🔑 Remember that criticism is also like a boomerang; give it, and you'll get it.

🔑 Pride is obnoxious to God.

🔑 Harmony in the home is absolutely essential.

🔑 Pleasant words set the tone for the day—and the life.

Chapter Thirteen

Invest Wisely and Profit

As God began to prosper our business, I took flying lessons and earned my pilot's license. I bought a single-engine Cessna 182. I was able to fly from Seattle to our businesses in Iowa, Idaho, and California. I enjoyed flying.

Then came one of the greatest challenges to my faith. It involved the purchase of a twin-engine airplane. Buying the airplane in 1964 was a tremendous step of faith. I flew into Omaha one day in my single-engine Cessna. The Cessna dealers there approached me saying, "Move up to a twin-engine plane. We have a special deal for you now." I listened to their presentation and quickly made the decision that a twin-engine plane was out of my league.

But, God surprises us at times. A few days later I was walking across the street in the little town of Glenwood, Iowa, where we owned a modern facility for the mentally retarded. As I stepped over the yellow line in the middle of the street, I heard the inner voice say unexpectedly, "Buy the twin-engine Cessna." *What?* I wasn't even thinking of the plane.

Instantly, I knew it was God's will. But I wondered, *How? It's impossible! I could never afford such a plane.*

Then I heard the Lord give me a figure of $41,000. The Cessna dealers were asking $52,000. *Could it be that they would accept such a lower offer?*

I called the salesman and told him I was interested. We met, and he was anxious to sell. He talked fast. Then I told him what I would pay. He looked hurt and said, "Don't be ridiculous." I told him my offer was final. He went to his supervisor, came back and said, "No deal." I walked out.

Two days later, the salesman called and said he was coming to see me. We met in a local restaurant, and he came down to $45,000. I said, "No deal." Suddenly, he slammed the pen on the table and said "Okay!" He took my offer, and I was happy.

Then we did the figures. The down payment would be my Cessna 182. Payments were to be $1,200 per month. *Oh,* I thought, *no way!* But that inner voice said, "Take it; I'll make a way." I also remembered my failure to buy the new Plymouth in unbelief. I didn't want to fail again.

So I signed the papers, took some lessons in the plane, and flew back to Seattle in a big, brand-new, twin-engine bird. On one occasion, I was privileged to fly Pastor John Osteen into Vera Cruz, Mexico, for a crusade. Pastor Osteen often referred later to that flight with me in his sermons on "overcoming fear."

This purchase was a huge step of faith. But, I could not have taken the challenge had I not acted in faith to God's inner voice in much smaller situations. I had learned to operate in faith with smaller challenges. So my faith had grown.

And, as a result of acting in faith, I received some unexpected benefits. Unknown to me, I learned that I could get a tax credit from the IRS and save about one-third of the price of the plane. I was allowed a business deduction for flying to our businesses, so I saved money there.

Not only that, because of my step of faith that pleased the Lord, we began to make more profit in the businesses. Empty beds in the nursing homes filled up. Income increased, and expenses were curbed. Soon, those monthly payments on the new plane were easy to make because of increased profits. We were even giving more to the kingdom of God. My faith kept growing.

Any action of faith on our part releases God to do the impossible. It causes Him to open His hand of blessing and provision. He will give supernatural increase. Faith pleases God.

Childlike faith moves God to act on our behalf. Furthermore, He provides abundantly.

I flew that plane for eight years. It was fun. I blessed pastors by taking them to the places they needed to go. I saved time traveling and saved money for the Lord's work.

Then one day I heard that same inner voice say, "Give the plane to your church for missionary work." *Wow!* It was still worth $30,000. *Give it away? Do without a plane?*

However, God had been so good to us, I knew I could trust Him. I was happy to give the plane to the Lord's work, especially after Marlene agreed that it was the thing to do.

We gave the plane to the Philadelphia Church in Seattle. It was to be used for missionary work in Africa. We were happy that we obeyed God.

As a result, our business flourished even more. We expanded by building two new convalescent homes in Iowa. And we continued to give.

Both the investment in the plane and the giving of it were major decisions. It was vital to know the will of God in those decisions. Had it not been God's will, the businesses would not have prospered. Knowing the will of God brings faith for the unseen. Marlene and I were in agreement on these decisions. We had peace—and faith because of it.

We Can Expect Good Things from the Lord

God is not stingy. He chooses to give us all things liberally. His Word says, "Command those who are rich in this present world not to be arrogant nor to put their hope in wealth, which is so uncertain, but to put their hope in God, who richly provides us with everything for our enjoyment. Command them to do good, to be rich in good deeds, and to be generous and willing to share" (1 Timothy 6:17-18 NIV).

Proverbs 28:25 NIV declares, "A greedy man stirs up dissension, but he who trusts in the Lord will prosper." In the same chapter, verse 27 says: "He who gives to the poor will lack nothing." The key here is to trust in God. Be humble. Be a giver.

God's warning is clear:

> People who want to get rich fall into temptation and a trap and into many foolish and harmful desires that plunge men into ruin and destruction. For the love of money is a root of all kinds of evil. Some people, eager for money, have wandered from the faith and pierced themselves with many griefs. But you, man of God, flee from all this, and pursue righteousness, godliness, faith, love, endurance and gentleness. Fight the good fight of the faith. Take hold of the eternal life to which you were called when you made your good confession in the presence of many witnesses. (1 Timothy 6:9-12 NIV)

We can expect the Lord to put good things into our hands. He wants us to enjoy them. Satan will constantly bring condemnation and guilt as we prosper. Don't accept the devil's accusations. *Guilt is one of his greatest deterrents to prosperity*. He will remind you of all those around you who don't have as much as you do. He will bring back scenes you have seen on TV of starving children. The usual response is to back off, reject the blessings God brings, and have nothing to help those very same people.

Enjoy what God has given you. Give Him the honor and thanks for it all. Ecclesiastes 5:19 confirms that when God gives a man wealth and possessions, the Lord enables him to enjoy them. In fact, as my son, Larry, and his wife testify below, finding joy in our work is a gift of God.

Larry and Laine's Testimony

"Faith is the substance of things hoped for" (Hebrews 11:1). Our hope was for a larger home closer to our church. Originally, we purchased a 1,400-square-foot home, which is a miracle story in itself. However, seven years, two children, and two home businesses later, we needed more space. The commute to our church was forty-five minutes each way, and we knew we needed to cut that time in half.

We looked in several locations for a new home, all of which appeared to be financially "out of our reach." We had recently gone to a Christian leader's conference during which God increased our faith for "double." So, we began praying, believing, and looking for twice as much as we were used to (i.e., square footage and mortgage payment).

We put our house up for sale. We patiently waited six months for a buyer with "evidence of things not yet seen." During that time God helped us know the exact area we were to move to. He also impressed upon us to be more specific in our prayers. So we listed out every detail of what our family needed and wanted.

Laine had a problem. What did she need and want? Having been driven by guilt, fear, and general anxiety her whole life, she was dealing

155

with an inner struggle. She said, "I knew, in my head, that God is a good God and wants to bless us. But I hadn't caught it in my spirit. Thoughts would arise: *Who do I think I am to have a larger, nicer home? Are we biting off more than we can chew? Am I being wasteful for having any extra space?* Wow, my own wrong thinking, what an obstacle! As I shared these thoughts with family and friends they helped break that stronghold by reminding me of God's true nature. He is a giving God who gave us His very best, His Son Jesus. He is a God of abundance who provides more than enough. His thoughts of me were more than the sand of the earth. God rejoices in the prosperity of His servants. I began to read the Word regarding these topics and praying God's Word over our situation. God's Word became the overriding thoughts I would choose to entertain. Wrong thinking quieted, and faith increased."

Laine continued, "Just when we thought we had our 'ducks in a row,' we got word that the major account in my business was soon to be discontinued. We had already qualified for our 'faith' house with our lender, but it depended heavily on that income. Common sense said, 'Hold on, stay where you are. You know you can make the current payments.' But God, in us, said, 'Go ahead. Step out in faith. That contract is not your source; I am your Source. Faith pleases Me.' So, Larry and I prayed together and agreed on God's will, and we sold our house."

Right away they found the house that met every detail on their list. Excitedly, they made an offer, but the offer was not accepted. They were down to the wire . . . by that time they had only one week to move out with no place to go.

The very next week a house became available in the exact location they wanted. As they walked into the entryway of that home, a peace came over both of them. Out loud they said, "This is it." Larry even named the price he was willing to pay. Walking through the house, they discovered that it was much better than any of the others they had tried to buy. They bought the house for the very amount Larry had determined. God worked it out for them.

The closing date was accelerated; they received surprise extra business, bonuses, and a refund from HUD. All costs were covered. God honored their trust and faith in Him. They both declare: "God is good. He is faithful." Faith wins out!

Speaking of houses as a good investment, here is what happened to me when I was feeling too old to invest.

Wise Investment—A House

In 1985, we moved from the country to Bellevue, Washington, near Seattle. We bought a lot with a great view of the city. I was fifty-five years old and ready to start retiring, when the Lord challenged us to move in faith. My natural mind was saying, *Don, you are too old to be building another big home costing $530,000. Use your head, your present home is debt free. This is stupid.*

But as Marlene and I prayed, we knew that building again was God's will for us. It was a new season in our lives. It was another step of faith, even though we were older. Faith has nothing to do with age. The only difference between the financial-related faith we needed when we were younger and the faith we need now is that today it usually involves more zeros. Actually, since we have built the house, our finances have increased. *How? Why?* Because faith pleases God. He wants to put more funds into our hands for His work.

God had plans we didn't understand at the time. We lived in that house four years. We enjoyed the view, hosted many friends, and had great ministry times there. I assumed that was the last big investment of my life. Wrong!

At the close of four years, we were led of the Lord to buy a lot across the street. We sold our new home; it had appreciated about $75,000. We sold it with a large equity to put into the new house.

Of course, now you know what I'm going to say. It was another step of faith. By then I was more than sixty years old, thinking, *Here we go again!*

Without more details, we built a new $700,000 home with a panoramic view of Mt. Rainier, the Cascade Mountains, Seattle, and the Olympic Mountains to the west.

What kind of investment was it? Twelve years later, our home was appraised at two million dollars. That is three times the cost! I am so happy that I didn't stay in the country relying on my own natural wisdom.

Today, we are giving more money to God than ever before. It doesn't make sense, but it is true. We have acted in faith, knowing the will of God. He knew ahead of time the value of the investment and the potential of financial strength. Thank God for His wisdom and direction in our investments.

Wealth Is for God's Work

In 1977, I was in Nairobi, Kenya, speaking to a group of businessmen. We were in the Hilton hotel. I had finished my speech when a young man approached me. He said, "I did not expect you, a businessman, to talk about God and the Bible. I did not think a Christian would be in the Hilton hotel."

He said that he always thought of businessmen as those who lived "high on the hog" at the expense of their employees. He had never connected business and the Bible. He thought the two were totally separate. He thought all businessmen lie and cheat, and he didn't think a Christian could ever be a businessperson.

That is too bad. He didn't understand how good God is to anyone who will believe and obey Him. He didn't stop to realize it was because God has prospered me that I could pay my fares and hotel bills to give him the "good news."

But I often hear someone question with surprise, "A businessman and the Bible? Church and business? What does the church have to do with sales or products?"

Money and spirituality are tied closely together, which seems to shock many people. God has much to say about our finances:

> Let them shout for joy and be glad, who favor my righteous cause; and let them say continually, "Let the LORD be magnified, who has pleasure in the prosperity of His servant." (Psalm 35:27 NKJV)

> Keep therefore the words of this covenant, and do them, that ye may prosper in all that ye do. (Deuteronomy 29:9)

> Humility and the fear of the LORD bring wealth and honor and life. (Proverbs 22:4 NIV)

The above verses are a statement of fact, more than a hopeful promise. It is a fact; our humility and obedience bring wealth, honor, and a rich, full life. How encouraging. What more could we want? These benefits of obedience encompass the whole of success in life.

In Proverbs 8, God promises lasting, durable wealth, not a fleeting flash of money for a while.[1] The Bible makes it clear that God wants His people to prosper.

As I said at the beginning of this book, dynamic faith, and its development, usually involves money. In business, we often have to move in faith. Those without faith might call it a gamble. But with God on our side directing us, it is not gambling. Good business is listening to God's voice and then acting like we believe Him, which means we will dare to do the unusual as He directs.

One of my best investments was in real estate in 1963. With four boys, we wanted to live in the country, and I had the opportunity to buy sixty-five acres in Fall City, Washington, just twenty-five miles east of Seattle. We bought the acreage and built a new home on it, overlooking the Snoqualmie River.

About a year later, I was looking at the description of my land. As I studied it, I found I did not have sixty-five acres but only fifty-two acres. I had paid for sixty-five acres. *What should I do?*

I met with the seller and shared with him the news about my shortage. He refused to acknowledge that I was short thirteen acres. I met with him twice, and there was no negotiation; he even refused to pay half of my loss.

Now I had a choice. I could legally go after him and sue him, or I could just let the matter drop. He was a neighbor, and I didn't want to fight him. Marlene and I prayed, asking the Lord what to do. His answer was, "Stay out of strife." To do that meant losing $15,000. As I prayed more, the Lord indicated that He would honor my staying out of strife. I dropped the matter, and lost the money. *But,* God was watching and absolutely honored my decision. About five years later, a big power company wanted to cross my property with a high-power line. In the negotiations and my approval, I was paid more than I had lost in the purchase of the land years before. Of course today that land has appreciated and is worth much more than I originally paid for it.

The lesson I learned was so valuable that in many situations later in life I had God's protection and provision because I avoided strife, even sometimes at personal humiliation. I would rather have God's blessing in the long run than a momentary sense of satisfaction.

We don't usually see God's plan of provision for the future, but He always blesses us if we honor Him in all things. As we honor Him, we begin to see the power and authority we have to "call the shots," so to speak, in all areas of life.

Profit through wise investments.

&— Investing in faith releases God to do the impossible.

&— Reject Satan's accusations when your investment succeeds.

&— Give God the honor and the credit for the increase.

&— Good stewardship involves wise investment.

&— Money and spirituality are vitally linked.

Millionaire Faith Key

Chapter Fourteen

Be Bold—Rule in Life

Once you have God-given wealth, you must learn to rule the business He gives you; don't let the business rule you. And don't be deceived into thinking it will run itself.

Predetermine the core values of your business according to biblical guidelines. You must "call the shots" according to God's leading. You set the standard of excellence. You establish the principles that govern the decisions of your business dealings. You predetermine success.

Jesus said, "Therefore I tell you, whatever you ask for in prayer, believe that you have received it, and it will be yours" (Mark 11:24 NIV). Knowing that we have that favor with God, we can ask for His protection in our business, and we can demand the devil to leave. We can take authority over Satan's activity and harassment. We can call a halt to his efforts to steal from us.

Several years ago, I used the power of this truth in a very practical way in my business. We were told that the state was requiring a financial audit for one of our nursing facilities. When my CPA called the state about it, he found that the state's strictest auditor was coming. My accountant told me this audit could cost us a lot of money.

But faith rose up inside of me. I said, "No. We have honored God, we have tithed, we haven't cheated, and we don't steal. Why should we lose money to the state for something that we haven't done?"

I told the administrator of our facility and the CPA to meet me before the auditor came. I said to them, "We are asking God to give us favor with this man. We will not lose money. It is God's work, and Satan is defeated."

We prayed, and I confessed, "No loss!"

The auditor finally came. He spent the entire day in our facility. When he called for the exit interview, everything seemed to be going very well. Then he said, "You have a problem in one area of this facility."

I saw my CPA cringe. *Here it comes*, I thought. But I was confessing under my breath, "No, Satan, no, you're not getting our money!"

The auditor continued by saying that we were filing one of our reports inaccurately.

My heart was saying, *No, no!*

Then he said, "I'll show you how to do this, because you have not been receiving all of the funds you are entitled to receive."

My CPA almost fell out of his chair. It was another miracle. The correction added more than a thousand dollars a month to our income in that facility.

Satan will steal from us every chance we give him. If we don't rule over him with God's promises, the devil will "eat our lunch." In that situation, we knew we had to obey God and stand against the enemy's attempts to steal our funds.

God has promised many benefits to those who obey Him. A man (or woman) of godly integrity obeys God. A man of godly character understands God's authority, recognizes the devil's attacks, and rules in his business. He can thwart the designs of Satan because he knows his own rights according to God's Word.

One of the areas I must contend for is a high occupancy in our facilities. Ten empty beds in any facility means no profit. When there are too many empty beds in any of our homes, I begin to take dominion. I know there are many people who need our care; the solution is to find them and help them find us. I dispatch the angels to go and bring in residents. I call the beds full in Jesus' name.

And when our profits are low, I tell Satan, "You're not stealing my money; get your hands off." I get aggressive. You must too. You can call a halt to the devil's theft and constant harassment. It is a spiritual battle, more than a business battle. If you don't stop him, the devil will "eat your lunch."

Do you need a better profit margin? Ask God for it and believe. If expenses get out of hand, ask God for wisdom and make the necessary adjustments to lower expenses. Rise up and say, "No, Satan, you're not stealing my money. I'm in charge here. This is my business, and I resist you. Get out!"

Keep Strife Rooted Out

Strife in any business will destroy it. We must rise up with indignation at actions and motives that are not pleasing to God. We must root out strife, calling a halt to it. We must believe for wisdom to terminate a person with a spirit of strife and a poor attitude.

There was a situation in one of our facilities in which two employees out of eighty were "badmouthing" us. Their actions were starting to influence the attitudes of others. When I found out about it, I immediately began to pray and take dominion. I said, "Lord, remove those two people; they must go."

Within three weeks, one quit, and the other had to move away because her husband was transferred to another city. My determination to rule over the situation, and the Lord's help, solved our problem.

If your business is failing, get some backbone and defy the devil. Thwart his designs against you. Take dominion in the affairs of your life and business.[1]

However, remember to submit yourself to God before you resist the devil.[2] Don't get that backward. Know God's Word and use it to rule over the devil and fend off his attacks against you.

The following list includes twenty leadership principles that I have taught to businessmen in many countries of the world. They are the core values that have been effective in ruling over my business.

I have already shared throughout this book many of the Scriptures that inspired the following guidelines, but I have included a few more Bible references in the endnotes for you to review as you meditate on these principles. I encourage you to take time to think about how each point applies to ruling over the work God has given you to do.

Twenty Core Values for Success in Life

1. Be assured that God wants you to prosper and succeed.[3]
2. Guide, guard, and govern your business; don't allow it to rule you.[4]
3. Rule your business through prayer (in the spiritual realm) and with common sense.
4. Pray for God's protection.
5. Seek godly counsel and advice.
6. Resist fear through knowledge of God's Word.[5]
7. Speak faith and success over your business and employees.[6]
8. Keep good records.

9. Know if you have a profit or loss.

10. Honor God with the tithe and offerings from your profit.

11. Demand honesty, diligence, and integrity in yourself and your employees.[7]

12. Give your employees lavish appreciation. Pay your employees well. You will attract better and more loyal employees.[8]

13. Keep your priorities right. Don't allow the business to rob you of quality time at home with your spouse and children.[9]

14. Maintain inner purity. Run from immorality; adultery will rob you of your profits.[10]

15. Find faithful, trustworthy people who will become able.[11]

16. Honor employees with fairness; no favoritism, no threats.[12]

17. Delegate authority, responsibility, and trust to your employees.

18. Expect excellence from yourself and your employees.

19. Be willing to change, or you will lose momentum and eventually your business will die.

20. Maintain an attitude of humility.[13]

You may not be the owner of a business as I am, but as an employee, or a pastor, or a professor, these same principles will work for you and cause you to be promoted, receive raises, and have favor with your employer and fellow employees.

Remember that character (both yours and those who work with you) is more important than talent and ability. The world looks for ability and talent before character, but God looks at the heart. The Word says, "Keep thy heart with all diligence; for out of it are the issues of life" (Proverbs 4:23).

As you obey God, your success will bring opportunities to lead others by your example. Encourage and teach those whom God places within your sphere of influence.

There's a Miracle in Your Mouth

Knowledge of God's promises gave me faith to rule over our business, which kept us from losing vast sums of money. Until you are willing to speak aloud and confess His promises, you will not receive the best God has for you.

I will elaborate on the power of your words in the next chapter. In order to reign and rule in life, it is important for you to realize the power of the tongue.

- Your words create prosperity or poverty.
- Your words bring health or sickness.
- Your words cause victory or defeat.
- Your words give God, or the devil, control of your life.

You will receive your miracle when you boldly confess the promises of God with your mouth. God's Word in your mouth is creative and anointed. God's Word in your mouth is as powerful as it was on the lips of Jesus. He will perform His Word (see Jeremiah 1:12).

Ruling with your God-given authority may not be easy at first. You may need to pray for faith and extra patience. But it will pay off, just as it did when we needed a miracle about our old building in Bremerton, Washington.

Speak to Your Mountains

For many years, we owned a hospital building that had been refurbished into a nursing home. It was a 51,000-square-foot building on four floors. As the years went by, it became too difficult and expensive to keep the building up to fire codes and health regulations. I decided to build a new nursing home and close the old building.

We wanted to sell the old building, but no one wanted it. I advertised it, listed it with a real estate agency, and did everything I could think of, but it didn't sell.

One day the Lord revealed to me that I had to speak to my mountain. That old building certainly was a mountain! It was costing me insurance, taxes, and security to the tune of nearly a thousand dollars per month. I decided to exercise my faith and speak to the old four-story building.

I got in my Cadillac and drove to the building. I stepped out of the car and pointed to the empty building and said, "Building, I call you sold in Jesus' name." I went to the other end of the building and said the same words. I went inside and repeated the same confession.

My insurance agent said, "You'll never sell that building." When I left his office, the devil whispered, "He's right; nobody will want that building."

I said out loud, "I call that building sold. Satan, you're a liar. I'm not listening to you, I'm listening to God!"

Marlene and I had to speak to that mountain for more than a year. We would not give in to any negative talk. We confessed that it was sold.

One day my administrator called and said, "Don, someone wants to buy your building." A few days later, I met him for lunch and sold the building. My mountain was gone.

I had to agree with the Word of God and refuse to listen to the devil. The miracle didn't come overnight, but it came. If we don't like what we have today, we must change our confession for the future.

I have often been asked to teach on why I have succeeded in business, so I made a list of the positive principles that I have confessed over my own life. I believe they will also help you rule in your life:

Ten Principles of Success Confessions

1. I am determined to know the will of God and obey Him.
2. I live by faith; I feed my faith regularly.
3. I watch my words; I refuse to talk the negative.
4. I receive wisdom from God by prayer and the Bible.
5. I rely on the Holy Spirit to guide, warn, and direct.
6. I tithe and give from my business and personal income.
7. I trust my employees and pay them well.
8. I take dominion over sin and Satan with his temptations.
9. I consider quality of care and service in business more important than profit.
10. I refuse worry and fear; I treat them like sin.

Never let trials, tests, and circumstances control your thoughts or confession of God's ability to overrule the circumstances of your life. Much of your authority depends on your knowledge of God's Word and the words that come out of your mouth.

The words you speak are important. Faith is vitally linked to your words; you can't say one thing and believe another. In the next chapter, I will show you how the words you speak may be limiting God. Faith-filled words are an important key to developing millionaire faith.

Be bold and rule in life.

- Rule in life by predetermined values and standards.

- Resist the devil's agenda to steal from you.

- Deal a deathblow to strife.

- Speak to your mountain; don't complain to God about it.

- Rely on the Holy Spirit to direct you.

Millionaire Faith Key

Chapter Fifteen

Speak to Your Mountains

In His Word God has made it clear that the words we choose make a difference, which is why He has instructed us to control them. His Word says, "From the fruit of his mouth a man's stomach is filled; with the harvest from his lips he is satisfied. The tongue has the power of life and death, and those who love it will eat its fruit" (Proverbs 18:20-21 NIV).

What kind of harvest will your words bring?

James wrote, "If anyone considers himself religious and yet does not keep a tight rein on his tongue, he deceives himself and his religion is worthless"(James 1:26 NIV). That Scripture reminds me of a story I read in Paul Yonggi Cho's book, *The Fourth Dimension.*[1] In the book, he tells of a neurosurgeon who had made a great discovery. He wrote:

> One morning I was eating breakfast with one of Korea's leading neuro-surgeons, who was telling me about various medical findings on the operation of the brain. He asked, "Dr. Cho, did you know that the speech center in the brain rules over all the nerves? You ministers really have power, because according to our recent findings in neurology, the speech center in the brain has total dominion over all the other nerves."

. . . Then this neuro-surgeon began to expound their findings. He said that the speech nerve center had such power over all of the body that simply speaking can give one control over his body, to manipulate it in the way he wishes. He said, "If someone keeps on saying, 'I'm going to become weak,' then right away, all the nerves receive that message, and they say, 'Oh, let's prepare to become weak . . .'"

"If someone says, 'Well, I have no ability. I can't do this job,' then right away all the nerves begin to declare the same thing. 'Yes,' they respond, 'we received instruction from the central nervous system saying that we have no abilities, to give up striving to develop any capacity for capability. We must prepare ourselves to be part of an incapable person.'"

"If someone keeps saying, 'I'm very old. I'm so very old, and am tired and can't do anything,' then right away, the speech central control responds, giving out orders to that effect. The nerves respond, 'Yes, we are old. We are ready for the grave. Let's be ready to disintegrate.' If someone keeps saying that he is old, then that person is soon going to die."

That neuro-surgeon continued saying, "That man should never retire. Once a man retires, he keeps repeating to himself, 'I am retired,' and all the nerves start responding and become less active and ready for a quick death."

This was not a spiritual principle with the surgeon, just a physical fact. He actually confirmed what the Word teaches: the tongue "corrupts the whole person, sets the whole course of his life on fire, and is itself set on fire by hell"

(James 3:6 NIV). Our words should be as David's who prayed, "May the words of my mouth and the meditation of my heart be pleasing in your sight, O LORD, my Rock and my Redeemer" (Psalm 19:14 NIV).

As we read in Mark 11:23, we can speak to problems the size of mountains, and they will be removed, if we believe in our heart that God's Word is true. Eventually we possess what we continually confess. It may not come in one day, one week, or one month, but it will come.

Jesus said: "Keep on asking and it will be given you; keep on seeking and you will find; keep on knocking [reverently] and [the door] will be opened to you. For everyone who keeps on asking receives; and he who keeps on seeking finds; and to him who keeps on knocking, [the door] will be opened" (Matthew 7:7-8 AMP).

We are simply to ask in faith. Then we are to speak words of faith and wait for the answer to our prayers. In this way, we will rule over our circumstances, bringing God's will to pass on earth.

Here is a promise upon which we can rely: "If you then, evil as you are, know how to give good and advantageous gifts to your children, how much more will your Father Who is in heaven [perfect as He is] give good and advantageous things to those who keep on asking Him!" (Matthew 7:11 AMP).

The woman with the issue of blood *said*, "If I just touch his clothes, I will be healed" (Mark 5:28 NIV). She was determined to push past her obstacles, and she got a miracle. We can do the same thing in our situation. If we do what people did in the Bible, we will get the same results they did.

My Words of Faith Were Tested

Many years ago, I noticed a small growth on my lower stomach. It kept growing, getting bigger and bigger. One day

Marlene saw it and said, "You should go to the doctor and have that taken off."

I thought about it for a few days and decided it was nothing to God to remove the growth. I decided to take authority over that ugly thing and command it to leave my body. I would lay my hand on it and say, "Get off my body. I curse you in the name of Jesus."

I did this for weeks, but didn't see any change. After about two months, I happened to look at my stomach. The growth was gone! I had to rule over my circumstances and persist in my determination to see that growth gone. I had to talk to it every day and not quit. As I did so, Jesus kept His Word and removed it.

During a crusade in 1969, I had the challenge of confessing healing contrary to physical feelings. We held a crusade in Cagayan de Oro City in the Philippines. I had invited evangelist John Osteen to minister there with us.

It was a great healing and evangelistic meeting. We saw eyes opened, goiters removed, and deaf ears opened. The meetings had been going for five days, when the devil attacked me with the flu.

The last meeting of the crusade was scheduled for a Sunday afternoon. I had been invited to speak that Sunday morning in a church about two hours from where we were staying. So Saturday evening I rode the bus to Iligan City. That night I started to ache all over; my back, legs, and head ached with pain.

The devil whispered and said, "You won't speak tomorrow."

That made me angry. I responded by saying out loud, "Yes, I will speak tomorrow. You are a liar." I then laid my hands on my body and commanded the pain to go. I said, "In Jesus' name, I am healed."

The voice came back, "You are not healed. You have pain in your body. You have the flu."

Satan will contest your victory every step of the way. Receiving healing is a battle with the devil.

I reaffirmed to the devil that I was healed, and then I went to sleep. The next morning I woke up, and I still ached all over. The devil came again saying, "I told you that you couldn't speak; you're sick."

I said, "I will speak, in Jesus' name."

I went to the meeting that morning aching all over, feeling so weak. However, as I walked to the platform and began to speak, I felt no pain. But as soon as I finished, the pain returned.

Satan was there, whispering in my ear again, "You are a phony. What a hypocrite. You are up there acting so great, and you are sick."

I refused to listen to him or agree with him. I replied, "With the stripes of Jesus I am healed. You were defeated by the blood of Jesus." I had to say it in faith, because I was still weak and hurting.

But I refused to give in to confessions of defeat.

The return trip was again two hours by bus. I was aching so much that I had John Osteen pray for me, but still there was no physical sign of relief. At 4:00 P.M. it was my duty to open the last meeting of the crusade.

I went, still weak, the devil still accusing me of being a fake. There I was in a healing crusade, and I was sick. But I acted on the promise of God. I opened the meeting by singing in the dialect, "Jesus Christ is the same yesterday and forever" (see Hebrews 13:8).

After about one minute of singing, I suddenly felt a warm presence cover me. It was like oil that flowed over my head, along my back, and down my legs. In less than a minute, I was totally free from all pain and weakness. I was healed! Satan was defeated. Oh, how I praised God! I can feel the praise even now.

It was a two-day battle. I had to confess my healing even though my body said I wasn't healed. I was determined to win. I was mad at the devil for harassing me. I am glad that I didn't give in and not go to the crusade because of the way I felt. That is the kind of faith and determination that we must maintain in order to rule over the work that God calls us to do.

Confession of the Word Will Always Win

It may be challenged, but God's power is greater than any other force. There may be delays that we don't understand, but we are not to change our confession while waiting for our prayers to be answered.

Be convinced and know in your heart that God will watch over His Word to perform it as He promises in Jeremiah 1:12. He will make His promises good. Rule over your circumstances with the same conviction and confession of Abraham who knew that God spoke of nonexistent things as if they already existed, as we see in Romans 4:17 AMP.

Paul said, "For if because of one man's trespass (lapse, offense) death reigned through that one, much more surely will those who receive [God's] overflowing grace (unmerited favor) and the free gift of righteousness [putting them into right standing with Himself] reign as kings in life through the one Man Jesus Christ (the Messiah, the Anointed One)" (Romans 5:17 AMP).

Rule in life. Don't let Satan push you around with fear and accusations. Doubt weakens your faith and limits what God can do for you. Don't speak words of doubt, saying that you are too young or too old, too weak or too tired, or that it is too soon or too late. Speak what God has spoken over you from His Word.

You will never be strong until you begin to say, "I am strong in the Lord" (see Joel 3:10).

You will lag behind until you say, day and night, "The Lord is the strength of my life" (Psalm 27:1).

If you are sick, boldly speak the promise from 1 Peter 2:24, saying, "I am healed by the stripes of Jesus."

If you are fearful, speak boldly the promise from Hebrews 13:6, saying, "The Lord is my helper; I will not be afraid."

If you are poor, speak from 3 John 2 saying, "I am prospering financially even as my soul prospers."

Tell the people you meet, "The Lord is my Provider. He is my Protector. He is my Provision."

Keep God's promises in your mouth. When you repeat God's Word, the power of His written words are the same as when they were spoken by Jesus and the apostles. Just remind yourself of God's promises. He loves you and wants to do for you what He has promised to you.

If people ask you how you feel, tell them *faith* has nothing to do with *feelings*. Tell them you agree with the promises from the Word of God. Tell them you believe the Word. Tell them what God's Word says, not how you feel, about your circumstances.

Don't make apologies for speaking the Word of God. Say, "I believe I receive. With Jesus' stripes I am healed. God has not given me the spirit of fear."

For example, in Isaiah 41:10 God exhorts us: "Fear thou not; for I am with thee: be not dismayed; for I am thy God: I will strengthen thee; yea, I will help thee; yea, I will uphold thee with the right hand of my righteousness." So you can boldly confess, "I am not afraid, because God is with me. He will help me. He strengthens me."

Know what God says, and then say specifically what it is you believe. Speak the Word. Let God's Word come out of your mouth and fill your conversation and plans.

It is important to understand the principles of being a good and faithful servant. I have purposefully repeated certain Scriptures throughout this book that need to be rooted in the foundation of your faith. By hearing and speaking them again and again, you will dispel any doubts of God's intention to bless you.

The core values and beliefs I have shared will guide you in recognizing God's voice and obeying His instruction as you develop millionaire faith for His purposes.

Key #15

Speak to your mountains.

⊶ The speech center in the brain affects the whole body.

⊶ Positive, pleasant words bring life and peace.

⊶ Speak faith, not doubt.

⊶ Speak the Word, not people's opinions or ideas.

⊶ Words are weapons; use them wisely.

Chapter Sixteen

Take Charge! Be a Winner!

I want you to enjoy the freedom to be a millionaire. To do so, I encourage you to review often the keys to millionaire faith that I am sharing with you. Don't be hesitant to take charge of your life. Put your trust in God's good plans to prosper you, and tell the devil to shut up.

As you learn to maintain good stewardship in your business, God will entrust more responsibility to our stewardship. I encourage you to read again the story in Matthew 25 of the three servants who were given stewardship of their master's money. The ones who invested their master's money wisely and earned great returns were rewarded and given even more, but the one who feared losing the money, the one who limited the master's grace and hid the money to keep it "safe," was considered evil and faithless.[1]

That story is foundational to understanding the principles of millionaire faith. I explained earlier in this book that the tithe belongs to the Lord; now it should seem clear that we are like the servants who have been given the Master's money to invest wisely on His behalf.

There is much work to be done in the kingdom of God. He is ready to give abundant funds to faithful servants who will obey His voice. I have written this book to convince believers that it is God's will for His people to succeed, to have money, and to prosper. And the purpose of prosperity is to advance the kingdom of God through the local church, missions, and evangelism outreaches.

Because God works through the local church, we believers must find a place of corporate worship and support a pastor. We all need a shepherd to help us in our walk of faith.

It is God's will that we encourage our pastors and give them support. We should talk to our pastors and ask for their advice. We should not fear them. It is vital to the success of God's kingdom work that we develop a church family of friends with good relationships. We should tithe and give regularly to the work of our church, responding to special project offerings such as buildings, missions, or equipment.

You can't be independent and critical and still serve God. Remain teachable and submissive to your pastor; be faithful to attend church services so you can grow in unity with God's vision for your local body of believers. Attend as many of the services as you can. Be there for prayer.

Offer to help with various functions such as ushering or operating the sound system, providing office help, or assisting with the offering. Don't just finance the work, but also get involved with the physical needs of church ministry.

And don't criticize the pastor for talking about money. Listen and receive with a positive attitude. Beware of greed and covetousness that may be stealing your joy. Anyone who dislikes the offering is usually greedy.

Continue to read good books on financial success and increase. Make your own list of prosperity verses. Memorize them. Adjust your way of thinking regarding finances and giving.

Remember, almost all growth in faith involves the giving of money. Plant your tithe (your seed) in good soil; God guarantees that your harvest will exceed your gift.

Be a Person of Valor

As we apply the principles of faith and speak God's Word into our circumstances, something dynamic happens in our spirit. A new authority comes into our life. A new boldness develops. We are transformed from frightened, whimpering cowards to courageous, fearless leaders.

We start to rise up like Gideon in the Bible. In Judges, we see Gideon cowering and afraid of the enemy—Gideon was a wimp. Even though an angel came and talked with him, he continued to whine. He questioned God's goodness. He said that God had forsaken His people. He complained that they never saw miracles anymore.[2]

Gideon was a mess. Yet God called him a man of valor.[3] Gideon saw himself as weak, needy, and poor. God saw him as strong, forceful, influential, and mighty. Although Gideon talked negatively about himself, God talked positively about him. God had plans to use him. Gideon finally agreed with God. The man of valor agrees with what God says about him and sees himself as strong, not weak.

The man (or woman) of valor is not a beggar, always pleading with God for help. He is dynamic, full of power. He takes charge. He steps out and leads with confidence. He says, "We are well able to do it. Let's go!"

The meaning of the Hebrew word translated *valor* is from another word meaning "a *force,* whether of men, means or other resources; an *army, wealth, virtue, . . . strength.*"[4] A person of valor is trained and able, like an army, or a company of soldiers with great force, goods, might, power, riches, and strength.

We too can become men and women of valor.

Characteristics of Godly Valor

First, the man of valor is strong in mind and spirit. The word *valor* is defined in the dictionary as "strength of mind or spirit that enables a person to encounter danger with firmness: personal bravery."[5] A man of godly valor walks in faith and bold authority. This faith and bold authority comes from the Word of God to him. He believes it. He accepts what God says about him, regardless of how he feels. This faith and bold authority also comes from a personal fellowship with the Father. The man of valor has an intimate relationship with God.

His faith is active, not passive. He is determined to see things happen. He doesn't sit around twiddling his thumbs, hoping for a change. He is aggressive. He is motivated. He contends for the anointing. He fights for victory and will not accept defeat.

The following story demonstrates valor at work in David as he defeated Goliath:

> And David spake to the men that stood by him, saying, What shall be done to the man that killeth this Philistine, and taketh away the reproach from Israel? for who is this uncircumcised Philistine, that he should defy the armies of the living God? . . . David said moreover, The LORD that delivered me out of the paw of the lion, and out of the paw of the bear, he will deliver me out of the hand of this Philistine. And Saul said unto David, Go, and the LORD be with thee . . .
>
> Then said David to the Philistine, Thou comest to me with a sword, and with a spear, and with a shield: but I come to thee in the name of the LORD of hosts, the God of the armies of Israel, whom thou hast defied . . . So David prevailed over the Philistine with a sling and with a stone, and smote the Philistine, and slew

him; but there was no sword in the hand of
David. (1 Samuel 17:26,37,45,50)

What a powerful man of faith and action! We can be
the same, defeating our enemy daily.

Second, the man of valor is a man of prayer. He spends
quality time with Jesus and the Word. His prayer life is
strong. He is specific in prayer. He prays in the Spirit. He
knows what he wants. Fellowship with God is more
important to him than any other relationship, but fellowship
with God always leads him to intercede for others. Prayer and
intercession produce confidence, faith, and power in his life.
His faith is developed in prayer.[6]

As a result of believing prayer, the man of valor
challenges the devil. He rebukes the enemy. He takes
dominion over Satan. He commands evil spirits to go. He
commands sickness to leave. He speaks life into his meetings
with others.

Third, the man of valor is filled with the Holy Spirit.
He sees with the eyes of the Spirit. As he prays in the Spirit,
he has a new anointing. He sees things not known in the
natural mind. He comprehends the mysteries of God, and
revelation comes to him as he studies God's Word. He knows
that his strength is from the Lord. Praying in the Spirit every
day, he builds himself up and relies on the power of the
indwelling Holy Spirit.[7]

Jesus Himself needed the power of the Holy Spirit.
Even though He was the Son of God, He was also the Son of
man. He was filled with the Holy Spirit (see Mark 1:10-11).
The Bible also says that He returned from the test in the
desert "in the power of the Spirit" (Luke 4:14).

The Lord Jesus commanded the disciples to go into all
the world—but not right away. He told them first to *stay* in
Jerusalem until they were filled with the Holy Spirit, to

receive power (see Luke 24:49). He knew that they could not make an impact or be victorious without the power of the Holy Spirit. They could not preach without the power of the Holy Ghost.

We must pray and believe for that power and anointing. *We must invite the Holy Spirit to help us.* We must thank Him and *continuously depend upon Him in order to live a godly life.* We must ask the Holy Spirit to work with us and in us. *He will come when invited. It is a great insult to ignore the Holy Spirit. Ask for His help.*

Jesus sent the Holy Spirit to us to take His place in our daily lives. In John 14:16, He said, "I will pray the Father, and he shall give you another Comforter, that he may abide with you for ever." In other words, "I am leaving, but the Holy Spirit will take My place on earth. He is the Chief Executor on the earth today."

The Holy Spirit is a wonderful, gentle person. He is real. He is God, the third person of the Holy Trinity. He wants to fellowship with us. He wants us to talk to Him, and He wants to talk with us in return. He has personality. He has come to act on behalf of Jesus and to reveal Jesus to us.

He is a wonderful Friend and Helper. God the Father is on the throne in heaven. God the Son is at the Father's right hand in heaven. God the Spirit is here with us on earth. He was sent to take Jesus' place and represent Jesus on earth.

In *The Amplified Bible* version of John 14:26 Jesus speaks of Him: "But the Comforter (Counselor, Helper, Intercessor, Advocate, Strengthener, Standby), the Holy Spirit, Whom the Father will send in My Name [in My place, to represent Me and act on My behalf], He will teach you all things. And He will cause you to recall (will remind you of, bring to your remembrance) everything I have told you."

Our measure of faith and power today is in direct proportion to our communion with Him. We hear His heart. We partake of His wisdom. We see His holiness and purity. The Holy Spirit makes us aware of sin and uncleanness. Living in sin dissipates the power and blessings of God in our lives, but drawing near to His Spirit causes us to hate sin in our lives.

A man of valor believes he has the power to accomplish whatever God tells him to do, because Jesus said to His disciples, "You shall receive power when the Holy Spirit has come upon you; and you shall be witnesses to Me in Jerusalem, and in all Judea and Samaria, and to the end of the earth" (Acts 1:8 NKJV).

The Greek word translated *power* in this verse is from another word meaning "force . . . ; specifically miraculous power (usually by implication, a miracle itself)." It is much like the Hebrew word translated *valor*. Jesus was saying that when the Holy Ghost comes upon us, we will receive "ability, abundance, meaning, might, . . . miracles, strength, . . . and mighty (wonderful) work."[8]

The Spirit-filled person of valor rises up and speaks out. He knows what God wants, and he acts on it. Even before it happens, he speaks of it as though it has already come to pass. He knows that God "gives life to the dead and calls things that are not as though they were" (Romans 4:17 NIV).

He doesn't see obstacles, shortage, or lack. Like Caleb, who looked confidently into the promised land, he says, "Let us go up at once, and possess it; for we are well able to overcome it" (Numbers 13:30).

A man of valor knows and values the anointing of the Holy Spirit in his life. He will not allow sin and uncleanness to dissipate the anointing. He makes a clean break with sin. He keeps his mind and spirit clean. He knows that he cannot live without the anointing and presence of the Holy Spirit.

Fourth, the man of valor is strong in his knowledge of the Word of God. He knows the Bible well. Because of this knowledge of the Bible, he knows what he believes. He is enthusiastic, positive, and persistent. He has vibrant faith. The Word of God is alive and meaningful to him. He believes God speaks to him as He did to Abraham, saying, "Is any thing too hard for the LORD?"(Genesis 18:14).

He sees himself as Joshua, who marched seven days around Jericho—not stopping until the walls of that city fell and he conquered it as God had instructed him.[9] The man of valor stands firm in faith as Joshua did, and he is victorious because he is persistent in his faith that God will keep His promise.

He can do this because he is filled with the Word of God. His faith is made alive and active as he studies and meditates on the Scriptures.

- He knows God's Word on healing and health.
- He knows God's Word regarding his financial plan.
- He knows God's Word giving direction to his life.

As a result of this knowledge:

- He marches out with boldness.
- He leads with confidence.
- He tears down strongholds with the help of the Lord.
- He goes forth boldly, confident that nothing is too hard for his God.

The man of valor fights and wins. He prospers and succeeds.

Believe and Receive

The life of faith is the only way to live. Expel thoughts of fear and lack. Your language as a believer should be, "I am a victor, not a victim. I can do all things with Christ. To me all things are possible. I refuse discouragement. I am full of faith, and it is still growing."

Make up your mind that you will not participate in recession! Plan for prosperity, because now you know that God delights in the prosperity of His servants. Think the thoughts of God. Your mind is a spiritual computer. Program it with the promises of the Bible by meditating on them diligently day and night!

Attack the spirit of poverty with faith in God's promises. Command that spirit of poverty to leave you. Confess as 3 John 2 exhorts, "I am prospering as my soul prospers." Refuse to be handicapped by poverty.

Confess that lack and shortage are no longer yours. Rise up and assert your authority over the devil and his thoughts. Speak to lack and shortage, saying, "Be gone! God is my Provider!"

Speak of nonexistent things as though they already exist. Speak prosperity even though it is not yet visible to the natural eye. Ignore your feelings and the reasoning of your mind. Focus on the promises of God. Decree your success. Command the devil to leave, confident that when you do so, he must flee.

Be firm in faith! Be strong in faith! Resist doubt! Declare that you have the same spirit of faith as that of the patriarchs of old. Declare with David when face to face with the giant, "Today I win! My God gives me the victory!" Satan will laugh at and try to intimidate you, just as Goliath laughed at young David. But just as Goliath fell before David, so you too will see your enemies defeated and scattered.

Let your motto be: "Believe and receive, or doubt and do without." Repeat that phrase until it is a part of your internal system.

Faith is not *trying* to believe. Faith never tries. Faith speaks. Faith commands. Faith expects. Faith receives. Faith refuses to compromise. Faith praises. Faith doesn't waver. Faith wins!

Feed your faith and starve your doubts. Climb that hill of success, knowing that you will reach the top. Be confident that your God cannot and will not fail. Join in the shout of faith, "We are well able to take the land. Let's go!" God will go with you. He will go before you. You will prosper for His purpose. Success is guaranteed!

Take charge of your life and be a winner!

- Good stewardship activates God's trust in you.

- Bless your local church with your attendance and finances.

- Challenge the devil and take dominion in your life.

- Invite the Holy Spirit to help you; if you ask, He will come.

- Be a believer and not a doubter!

Keys to Millionaire Faith

Key # 1:   Leave your comfort zone.

Key # 2:   Be blessed to be a blessing to others.

Key # 3:   Tithe from your estimated increase.

Key # 4:   Just get up and grow!

Key # 5:   Feed your faith and starve doubt.

Key # 6:   Trust God to give you His best.

Key # 7:   Expect miracles when you obey God.

Key # 8:   Invest 10 percent of your income in God's work.

Key # 9:   Give generously to guarantee prosperity.

Key #10:   Defy logic and push the envelope.

Key #11:   Guarantee success through integrity.

Key #12:   Be a person of godly character.

Key #13:   Profit through wise investments.

Key #14:   Be bold and rule in life.

Key #15:   Speak to your mountains.

Key #16:   Take charge of your life and be a winner!

NOTES

CHAPTER 1

1. See Titus 1:7-8: For a bishop must be blameless, as the steward of God; not selfwilled, not soon angry, not given to wine, no striker, *not given to filthy lucre*; but a lover of hospitality, a lover of good men, sober, just, holy, temperate. (italics mine) *Lucre* is translated as "dishonest gain" in 1 Timothy 3:8 NIV: Deacons, likewise, are to be men worthy of respect, sincere, not indulging in much wine, and not pursuing *dishonest gain*. (italics mine)

2. See Mark 10:24-27 NIV: The disciples were amazed at his words. But Jesus said again, "Children, how hard it is to enter the kingdom of God! It is easier for a camel to go through the eye of a needle than for a rich man to enter the kingdom of God." The disciples were even more amazed, and said to each other, "Who then can be saved?" Jesus looked at them and said, "With man this is impossible, but not with God; all things are possible with God."

CHAPTER 2

1. James Strong, *Strong's Exhaustive Concordance of the Bible* (Nashville: Holman Bible Publishers, 1994), s.v. *money*; mammonas (*mam-mo-nas'*), reference 3126.

2. Derek Prince, *God's Plan for Your Money* (New Kensington, PA: Whitaker House, 1995), p. 18.

3. Romans 4:16-17 NIV: Therefore, the promise comes by faith, so that it may be by grace and may be guaranteed to all Abraham's offspring—not only to those who are of the law but also to those who are of the faith of Abraham. He is the father of us all. As it is written: "I have made you a father of many nations." He is our father in the sight of God, in whom he believed—the God who gives life to the dead and calls things that are not as though they were.

4. Kenneth E. Hagin, *Faith Food Devotions* (Tulsa: Kenneth Hagin Ministries, 1996), p. 126.

CHAPTER 3

1. See Proverbs 4:20-22 NIV: My son, pay attention to what I say; listen closely to my words. Do not let them out of your sight, keep them within your heart; for they are life to those who find them and health to a man's whole body.
2. Kenneth E. Hagin, *Exceedingly Growing Faith* (Tulsa: Kenneth Hagin Ministries, 1983), p. 13.
3. W. E. Vine, Merrill F. Unger, William White Jr., *Vine's Complete Expository Dictionary of Old and New Testament Words* (Nashville: Thomas Nelson, Inc., 1984, 1996), s.v. WORD: LOGOS . . . denotes (I) the expression of thought—not the mere name of an object—*(a)* as embodying a conception or idea . . . *(b)* a saying or statement . . . , the revealed will of God . . . RHEMA . . . denotes that which is spoken, what is uttered in speech or writing [used in Rom. 10:17 ("faith cometh by hearing, and hearing by the *word* of God")] . . . The significance of *rhema* (as distinct from *logos*) is exemplified in the injunction to take "the sword of the Spirit, which is the word of God," Eph. 6:17; here the reference is not the whole Bible as such, but to the individual scripture which the Spirit brings to our remembrance for use in time of need, a prerequisite being the regular storing of the mind with Scripture.

CHAPTER 4

1. See 1 Corinthians 2:16: For who hath known the mind of the Lord, that he may instruct him? But we have the mind of Christ.

CHAPTER 5

1. See Matthew 9:20-22: And, behold, a woman, which was diseased with an issue of blood twelve years, came behind him, and touched the hem of his garment: For she said within

herself, If I may but touch his garment, I shall be whole. But Jesus turned him about, and when he saw her, he said, Daughter, be of good comfort; thy faith hath made thee whole. And the woman was made whole from that hour.

2. See Matthew 8:8-10: The centurion answered and said, Lord, I am not worthy that thou shouldest come under my roof: but speak the word only, and my servant shall be healed. For I am a man under authority, having soldiers under me: and I say to this man, Go, and he goeth; and to another, Come, and he cometh; and to my servant, Do this, and he doeth it. When Jesus heard it, he marvelled, and said to them that followed, Verily I say unto you, I have not found so great faith, no, not in Israel.

CHAPTER 6

1. See Romans 4:17: (As it is written, I have made thee a father of many nations,) before him whom he believed, even God, who quickeneth the dead, and calleth those things which be not as though they were.
2. Strong, s.v. *health*; marpe' (*mar-pay'*), reference 4832.

CHAPTER 8

1. Strong, s.v. *consider;* katanoeo (*kat-an-o-eh'-o*), reference 2657.

CHAPTER 9

1. See Hebrews 11:6: But without faith it is impossible to please him: for he that cometh to God must believe that he is, and that he is a rewarder of them that diligently seek him.

CHAPTER 13

1. See Proverbs 8:17-18 NAS: "I love those who love me; and those who diligently seek me will find me. Riches and honor are with me, enduring wealth and righteousness."

CHAPTER 14

1. See Romans 5:17 NIV: For if, by the trespass of the one man, death reigned through that one man, how much more will those who receive God's abundant provision of grace and of the gift of righteousness reign in life through the one man, Jesus Christ.

2. See James 4:7-8: Submit yourselves therefore to God. Resist the devil, and he will flee from you. Draw nigh to God, and he will draw nigh to you.

3. See Proverbs 8:21 NKJV: That I may cause those who love me to inherit wealth, that I may fill their treasuries.
   See also Deuteronomy 29:9 NIV: Carefully follow the terms of this covenant, so that you may prosper in everything you do.
   See also Joshua 1:7-8 NIV: Be strong and very courageous. Be careful to obey all the law my servant Moses gave you; do not turn from it to the right or to the left, that you may be successful wherever you go. Do not let this Book of the Law depart from your mouth; meditate on it day and night, so that you may be careful to do everything written in it. Then you will be prosperous and successful. Have I not commanded you? Be strong and courageous. Do not be terrified; do not be discouraged, for the LORD your God will be with you wherever you go.
   See also Psalm 1:1-3 NAS: How blessed is the man who does not walk in the counsel of the wicked, nor stand in the path of sinners, nor sit in the seat of scoffers! But his delight is in the law of the LORD, and in His law he meditates day and night. And he will be like a tree firmly planted by streams of water, which yields its fruit in its season, and its leaf does not wither; and in whatever he does, he prospers.

4. God commanded man to have dominion and rule the earth: See Genesis 1:28: And God blessed them, and God said unto them, Be fruitful, and multiply, and replenish the earth, and subdue it: and have dominion over the fish of the sea, and over the fowl of the air, and over every living thing that moveth upon the earth.

5. See Isaiah 41:10 NKJV: "Fear not, for I am with you; be not dismayed, for I am your God. I will strengthen you, yes, I will help you, I will uphold you with My righteous right hand."

   See also 2 Timothy 1:7: For God hath not given us the spirit of fear; but of power, and of love, and of a sound mind.

6. See Mark 11:23-24 NIV: "I tell you the truth, if anyone says to this mountain, 'Go, throw yourself into the sea,' and does not doubt in his heart but believes that what he says will happen, it will be done for him. Therefore I tell you, whatever you ask for in prayer, believe that you have received it, and it will be yours."

   See also Proverbs 18:21: Death and life are in the power of the tongue: and they that love it shall eat the fruit thereof.

7. See Proverbs 12:24 NIV: Diligent hands will rule, but laziness ends in slave labor.

8. See James 5:4 NIV: Look! The wages you failed to pay the workmen who mowed your fields are crying out against you. The cries of the harvesters have reached the ears of the Lord Almighty.

   See also Malachi 3:5: And I will come near to you to judgment; and I will be a swift witness against the sorcerers, and against the adulterers, and against false swearers, and against those that oppress the hireling in his wages, the widow, and the fatherless, and that turn aside the stranger from his right, and fear not me, saith the LORD of hosts.

9. See Matthew 6:33: But seek ye first the kingdom of God, and his righteousness; and all these things shall be added unto you.

   See also 1 Timothy 5:8: But if any provide not for his own, and specially for those of his own house, he hath denied the faith, and is worse than an infidel.

10. See Proverbs 5:3-10 NAS: For the lips of an adulteress drip honey, and smoother than oil is her speech; but in the end she is bitter as wormwood, sharp as a two-edged sword . . . She does not ponder the path of life; her ways are unstable, she does not know it. Now then, my sons, listen to me, and do not depart from the words of my mouth. Keep your way far from her, and

do not go near the door of her house, lest you give your vigor to others, and your years to the cruel one; lest strangers be filled with your strength, and your hard-earned goods go to the house of an alien.

See also Proverbs 6:32 NIV: But a man who commits adultery lacks judgment; whoever does so destroys himself.

See also 1 Thessalonians 4:3-7 NIV: It is God's will that you should be sanctified: that you should avoid sexual immorality; that each of you should learn to control his own body in a way that is holy and honorable, not in passionate lust like the heathen, who do not know God; and that in this matter no one should wrong his brother or take advantage of him. The Lord will punish men for all such sins, as we have already told you and warned you. For God did not call us to be impure, but to live a holy life.

11. See 2 Timothy 2:2 NKJV: And the things that you have heard from me among many witnesses, commit these to faithful men who will be able to teach others also.

12. See Ephesians 6:9: And, ye masters, do the same things unto them, forbearing threatening: knowing that your Master also is in heaven; neither is there respect of persons with him.

    See also Colossians 4:1: Masters, give unto your servants that which is just and equal; knowing that ye also have a Master in heaven.

    See also Proverbs 19:17: He that hath pity upon the poor lendeth unto the LORD; and that which he hath given will he pay him again.

13. See Philippians 2:3 NKJV: Let nothing be done through selfish ambition or conceit, but in lowliness of mind let each esteem others better than himself.

    See also Proverbs 15:23: A man hath joy by the answer of his mouth: and a word spoken in due season, how good is it!

    See also Proverbs 18:12 NKJV: Before destruction the heart of a man is haughty, and before honor is humility.

See also Proverbs 22:4 NKJV: By humility and the fear of the LORD are riches and honor and life.

CHAPTER 15

1. Paul Yonggi Cho, *The Fourth Dimension* (Plainfield, NJ: Logos Int'l., 1979), adapted from pp. 67-69.

CHAPTER 16

1. See Matthew 25:14-18, 26-28: For the kingdom of heaven is as a man travelling into a far country, who called his own servants, and delivered unto them his goods. And unto one he gave five talents, to another two, and to another one; to every man according to his several ability; and straightway took his journey. Then he that had received the five talents went and traded with the same, and made them other five talents. And likewise he that had received two, he also gained other two. But he that had received one went and digged in the earth, and hid his lord's money . . . His lord answered and said unto him, Thou wicked and slothful servant, thou knewest that I reap where I sowed not, and gather where I have not strawed: Thou oughtest therefore to have put my money to the exchangers, and then at my coming I should have received mine own with usury. Take therefore the talent from him, and give it unto him which hath ten talents.

2. See Judges 6:13: And Gideon said unto him, Oh my Lord, if the LORD be with us, why then is all this befallen us? and where be all his miracles which our fathers told us of, saying, Did not the LORD bring us up from Egypt? but now the LORD hath forsaken us, and delivered us into the hands of the Midianites.

3. See Judges 6:12: And the angel of the LORD appeared unto him, and said unto him, The LORD is with thee, thou mighty man of valour.

4. Strong, s.v. valor; chayil (*khah'-yil*); reference 2428.

5. *Merriam Webster's Collegiate Dictionary, Tenth Edition*, s.v. "valor."

6. See Hebrews 11:6: But without faith it is impossible to please him: for he that cometh to God must believe that he is, and that he is a rewarder of them that diligently seek him.

7. See 1 Corinthians 14:2-4,14-15: For he that speaketh in an unknown tongue speaketh not unto men, but unto God: for no man understandeth him; howbeit in the spirit he speaketh mysteries. But he that prophesieth speaketh unto men to edification, and exhortation, and comfort. He that speaketh in an unknown tongue edifieth himself; but he that prophesieth edifieth the church . . . For if I pray in an unknown tongue, my spirit prayeth, but my understanding is unfruitful. What is it then? I will pray with the spirit, and I will pray with the understanding also: I will sing with the spirit, and I will sing with the understanding also.

8. Strong s.v. power; dunamis (*doo'-nam-is*); reference 1411.

9. See Joshua 6:1-19: So the people shouted when the priests blew with the trumpets: and it came to pass, when the people heard the sound of the trumpet, and the people shouted with a great shout, that the wall fell down flat, so that the people went up into the city, every man straight before him, and they took the city (v. 20).

ABOUT THE AUTHOR

Don is the owner of eight convalescent facilities in Washington and California, where he has directed a profitable business for more than forty years. His facilities offer quality care to more than five hundred residents each day and employ nearly four hundred superior staff members.

To Don, success and prosperity are expected, however, with a definite purpose. His goal is to serve people and to use finances for the kingdom of God. The best principles for success are in the Bible, which Don calls "The Success Manual."

Because of continued success in the business, Don has been able to travel to sixty-nine countries, speaking and teaching in conventions, conferences, and churches. He has actively served on several boards, reaching businessmen around the world. He is an elder and is active in the ministries of The City Church, in Kirkland, Washington.

AUTHOR CONTACT INFORMATION

For additional copies of this book contact your local bookstore
or write to:

Don Ostrom

The City Church

9051 132nd Ave. NE

Kirkland, WA 98033

Phone: 425.803.3233

Fax: 425.889.8940

E-mail: cityinfo@thecity.org

Web site: www.thecity.org